The Islamic State
A Brief Introduction

CHARLES R. LISTER

D1016049

BROOKINGS INSTITUTION PRESS
Washington, D.C.

The Brookings Institution is a private nonprofit organization devoted
to research, education, and publication on important issues of domestic
and foreign policy. Its principal purpose is to bring the highest quality
independent research and analysis to bear on current and emerging policy
problems. Interpretations or conclusions in Brookings publications should
be understood to be solely those of the authors.

Library of Congress Cataloging-in-Publication data is available.
ISBN 978-0-8157-2667-8

9 8 7 6 5 4 3 2 1

Printed on acid-free paper

Typeset in Sabon and Meta

Composition by Cynthia Stock
Silver Spring, Maryland

Contents

Foreword
AHMED RASHID

THE GREATEST POSSIBLE threat to stability in the Middle East and the wider Muslim world in the modern era has been the unrelenting conquests and destruction of borders by the Islamic State in Iraq and al-Sham (ISIS), later declared as the Islamic State (IS). As an inspirational force it has been equally successful in mobilizing young Muslims worldwide. Not since Arab Muslim armies spread out to conquer the world in the aftermath of the death of the Prophet Muhammad in the seventh century have we witnessed such a powerful force that has combined brilliant military and political strategy along with abject cruelty and oppression of those who are under its thrall.

Yet unlike those early armies, ISIS conquests have been carried out with horrendous massacres, executions, and the killing of tens of thousands of civilians, forced conversions, and literal modern-day enslavement of minorities and women—if they are not immediately killed. Yet such is the inspirational power of ISIS and the Islamic State that more than 18,000 Muslims from ninety countries have joined its ranks as of this writing.

Contrary to much Western analysis, ISIS has generated a civil war *within* Islam, exacerbating the Sunni-Shia rift by its call to eliminate all Shias; declaring as *takfir*—unacceptable and liable to be killed—all those Sunnis who do not follow ISIS's particular creed of Islam, which is based on a variant of Wahabbism; and destroying the idea of pluralistic Muslim societies in the Middle East, most of which have accommodated religious and ethnic minorities—Christians, Jews, Yazidis, Druze, and Kurds—since before the time of the Prophet Muhammad.

For the moment at least ISIS is not waging a war against the West. This makes it essentially different from al-Qaeda, whose original aim was to topple Western capitalism so that the Arab world could then more easily fall into its hands. While al-Qaeda sought to destroy the far enemy in order to eventually topple the near enemy of Arab rulers, ISIS has a totally different approach, believing that political power and territory must first be won in the Middle East. Nor is ISIS a nationalist-jihadist movement such as the Taliban of Afghanistan or even al-Shabab in Somalia, which restricts its aims and methodology to eliminating the old establishment and creating a new sharia state in one nation.

Although ISIS's followers have been carrying out individual acts of terrorism in the West, such as the recent, ISIS-inspired attacks in France and Canada, the movement does not advocate a strategic war against the West, nor is it known to be planning a 9/11-style terrorist attack on a major Western city. ISIS decapitations of Western journalists and aid workers, brutal as these acts have been, are not a declaration of war but rather acts of revenge for the deaths of its own fighters at the hands of American and coalition bombing and an attempt to terrify Westerners and locals into submission. One sign of its reluctance to take on the West for the moment is its refusal to launch terrorist attacks against Israel or propagate against that country. Nor did ISIS openly side with the Palestinians during the 2014 Israeli-Palestinian war in Gaza, as did other Arabs.

ISIS is determined to build a unitary state, or caliphate, that eliminates all borders in the Middle East and to extend those borders even further—as far as India and Central Asia. Unlike suicide bombers from other groups who wish to attain martyrdom and paradise in heaven, ISIS wants to also build a paradise on earth. In the theory and practice of state building it has gone many steps further than other groups. Even as it has eliminated educated Muslims who do not follow its creed, it has tried to enlist fellow extremists who have skills, education, and administrative abilities to join its state-building experiments in the territory it controls. Thus, it is more advanced than al-Qaeda, which left the need for state building far into the future. Nor is ISIS in the mold of the Taliban, which mistrusted all Muslim technocrats when it ruled Afghanistan between 1996 and 2001. As a consequence, the Taliban state was on the verge of collapse well before the U.S. invasion of 2001.

Even more detrimental than the elimination of borders such as those between Syria and Iraq is the ISIS war against minorities and women, which is becoming genocidal. If left to run its course, the group could utterly destroy 4,000 years of history in the Middle East—a region that has seen the birth of three of the world's most followed religions and countless prophets and has always been a rich and wonderful tapestry of different cultures, beliefs, and ethnicities. The 1 million Christians who lived in Iraq in 2003 are now reduced to less than a quarter of that number, while half a million Assyrians who speak Aramaic—the language of Jesus Christ—have fled from Iraq, as have Armenians and Greeks. Minorities in Syria have suffered even more: more than 200,000 people have been killed in the past four years. To render the entire Middle East only for those Muslims who follow the ISIS creed is nothing less than a war on the world's religions and history.

ISIS's success has been enhanced by several factors. The first has been its mastering of three forms of warfare that together no Arab army or other extremist group has the capacity to match. With the capture of American heavy artillery, missiles, and tanks from the Iraqi army, it has understood the art of conventional war, laying siege to cities, attacking targets en masse, or concentrating forces on several targets at the same time—be they in Syria or Iraq. With enhanced mobility from machine gun–mounted pickups and motor bikes, its forces can also fight a sustained guerrilla war to harass its enemies over long stretches of desert, and with the use of suicide bombings and mass executions, it has taken acts of terrorism to a new level.

Although some of these tactics have been adopted from the Taliban, al-Qaeda, and other groups, no extremist force has used such a wide array of military tactics within what appears to be an overarching strategic plan. As Charles Lister writes, this has been made possible in part by the recruitment of 1,000 or more regular army officers from the very Iraqi army that the Americans disbanded a decade ago. Many of the ISIS top commanders are former Iraqi officers, now disenfranchised and alienated from the state.

Equally unrelenting has been ISIS's ability to spread its message around the world using social media, while limiting the ability of the world media and intelligence agencies to know what is going on in ISIS-controlled territory. It allows only media coverage that it broadcasts itself. By executing American journalists, it has ensured that no independent journalist will have access to the state that ISIS is attempting to build.

In addition, ISIS has quickly become the richest terrorist force in history due to its capture of oil wells, use of kidnappings for ransom, bank robberies, and taxes from businesses and shops under its control. It has millions of dollars in income at its disposal to pay for fighters, social services, and state-building efforts. The West and Arab allies have been able to do little to dent ISIS influence in social media or its fundraising abilities.

Ultimately, ISIS's growth has not depended on its skills or ruthlessness, but on the distinct political and military vacuum in Syria, a result of the ruinous four-year-long civil war, and in Iraq, a result of the alienation of the Sunni population by the government of former prime minister Nuri al-Maliki. Underlying these conditions has been the failure of the Western occupation force in Iraq to carry out effective nation building after the U.S. invasion.

Before it pulled its forces out, the United States failed to leave behind sustainable democratic institutions, a well-trained army, a functioning bureaucracy, and relative ethnic and sectarian harmony. Unfortunately, the legacy of

U.S. intervention in Iraq is mirrored in Afghanistan and even more in Libya, where, after providing military force to oust Muammar Gaddafi, the United States did not follow up to help build a new government.

These actions, or the lack of them, have helped create the basis for intense hatred of the United States in the Arab street, which ISIS has benefited from enormously. However, the Arab world is deeply polarized. While anti-Americanism is likely to spread further with the U.S. bombing of ISIS targets, many Arabs still believe that only the American military can save them from ISIS's clutches. Anti-Americanism in the wider Muslim diaspora has certainly become a factor helping create the rush of young Muslims around the world wanting to enlist in ISIS.

Charles Lister has contributed enormously to our understanding of ISIS and recent events in the Arab world with *The Islamic State: A Brief Introduction*. He has shown that ISIS is not a short-term aberration in the Arab world but has deep ideological and social roots in Iraq that go back to the period well before the U.S. invasion and to the growth of al-Qaeda in Afghanistan and Pakistan. Lister also helps us understand what ISIS wants, which is only the first step in knowing what is needed to destroy it.

I believe that in accepting these premises about ISIS—that it is a single-minded force determined to establish its hegemony no matter the cost—we require a different kind of strategy than that which the United States is pursuing at the moment. First, the Arab states should be leading the present coalition and not Washington. By taking on a leadership role the United States is only reminding Arabs and Muslims of its past failures in Iraq, Libya, and Afghanistan and encouraging anti-Americanism. The United States is clearly vital for the success of the coalition of nations countering ISIS and especially in coordinating military action, but its real role should be preparing the Arabs to assume leadership of the coalition. This requires a huge diplomatic investment by the United States that is not apparent at the moment.

The Arab world itself is deeply divided. Before any success against ISIS can be notched up, there is a vital need to galvanize greater political unity among the Arab states so that their differences are reduced, they cooperate better with one another, and together they play a more important military role in defeating ISIS. Moreover, the rift between the Arabs and Iran will have to be mended. Iran has to play a vital role in helping to defeat ISIS, but it can do so only alongside the Arab world, not in opposition to it. Such a rapprochement would also help heal the present Shia-Sunni rift.

Education is key here. Arab states must develop a common narrative to counter extremism and address the need for a moderate interpretation of Islam through more modern educational curricula. Only radical steps taken by Arab regimes can stem the tide of young people being influenced by ISIS. Yet there is no sign of that awareness at present among Arab leaders.

ISIS is already knocking on the doors of Lebanon, Jordan, Saudi Arabia, and shortly the Gulf states. Arab regimes must collectively agree on a course of action if ISIS is to be defeated, extremism extinguished, and a tolerant Islam encouraged in the region. The United States and NATO need to prepare the ground for that to happen with intense diplomatic activity, going beyond the overwhelming obsession that the United States has shown for using military options. ISIS must be defeated militarily, politically, and diplomatically. Nothing else will do. *The Islamic State* is the best basic understanding available of the ISIS phenomenon and how to deal with it.

Lahore
January 2015

Acknowledgments

THE INSIGHT AND detail that I have gained through my travels in the Levantine region have been of particular value in writing this book, and they have been complemented by my contact and dialogue with others working on Syria, Iraq, Lebanon, and Turkey as well as on the subject of jihadi militancy. I am grateful for insights gleaned from conversations with, to name but a few, Aaron Zelin, Will McCants, Shadi Hamid, Emile Hokayem, Aaron Stein, Hassan Hassan, Noah Bonsey, Andrew Tabler, Raffaello Pantucci, Aron Lund, Usama Hassan, J. M. Berger, Mitchell Prothero, and Bilal Abdul Kareem. This, of course, is not to mention countless friends and colleagues within the governments of the United Kingdom, the United States, Canada, the Netherlands, and Norway, who have the immensely challenging task of dealing with this issue on the policy side.

I would also like to thank all my colleagues at the Brookings Doha Center (BDC) for their immediate backing and consistent support of this volume. Specifically, I would like to thank BDC director Salman Shaikh for his generous and consistent support. Our extensive work together engaging with Syrian insurgent groups has proven invaluable in my wider assessment of the conflict. I'm also extremely grateful to BDC director of research Sultan Barakat, who provided indispensable feedback and guidance during the drafting of the manuscript. Work done by Vittoria Federici and Bill Hess in constructively editing the manuscript was impressively efficient. Notable thanks must also go to the BDC communications department for its invaluable work in translating, formatting, publishing, and promoting the work.

Finally, I thank my wife, Jessica, for her endless patience, care, and understanding throughout my seemingly unending periods of research and travel.

More than a Terrorist Organization

THE THREAT POSED by Sunni jihadis has been evolving for at least the past two decades. While the late 1980s and 1990s witnessed the emergence of the notoriously transnationally minded al-Qaeda organization, the 2005–10 period saw al-Qaeda's regionally dispersed affiliates focused on establishing local bases of operations and acquiring and consolidating territorial control from which to launch more expansive attacks on the "near enemy," meaning local governments. Although terrorist plots against Western targets have continued to emerge, the principal threat to Western interests today lies in the Middle East's increasing instability, which jihadi groups have exploited for their own benefit.

This instability stretches across Iraq, Syria, and Lebanon and encompasses the border regions of southern Turkey and northern Jordan. While the militarization of the Syrian revolution from mid-2011 has played a critical role in destabilizing the region, the most significant risk to its long-term stability springs from the vision espoused by jihadis known after 2013 as the Islamic State in Iraq and the

Levant (ISIL), also as the Islamic State in Iraq and al-Sham (ISIS). On June 29, 2014, the first day of the Islamic holy month of Ramadan, ISIS spokesman Taha Subhi Falaha (Abu Muhammad al-Adnani) announced the restoration of the caliphate under the leadership of Ibrahim Awwad Ibrahim Ali al-Badri al-Samarra'iyy (Abu Bakr al-Baghdadi). Adnani declared the group would henceforth be known as the Islamic State (IS) and Baghdadi as "Caliph Ibrahim." This bold move came just weeks after ISIS had seized Iraq's second-largest city, Mosul, on June 10, thereby dramatically inflaming the armed Sunni uprising against the government of Nuri al-Maliki. Meanwhile, ISIS was also on the offensive in eastern Syria and consolidating its hold over the area surrounding the northern city of Raqqa, the group's capital. Consequently, by the time Caliph Ibrahim made his first public appearance on July 4, IS controlled territory stretching from al-Bab in Syria's Aleppo Governorate to Suleiman Bek in Iraq's Salah ad Din Province, over 400 miles away.[1]

Before seizing Mosul in June, ISIS retained assets likely nearing at least $875 million.[2] By September the figure was closer to perhaps $2 billion—that is, if judged by the scale of American-made Iraqi military equipment the group had captured and an estimated $2 million a day earned through smuggling oil from Iraq and Syria, among other revenue streams—turning the group not only into the wealthiest terrorist organization in the world but also into a formidable militant organization.[3]

An impressively managed, almost obsessively bureaucratic organization, IS has become a serious threat to both regional and international security, not to mention a challenge to al-Qaeda as the recognized leader of transnational jihadism capable of attracting recruits from across the globe. The scale of this threat was reflected in the airstrikes initiated in August 2014 by the United States and its coalition partners aimed at containing, degrading, and eventually destroying IS in Iraq and Syria. While such international pressure has at least partially forced IS to move underground, the group has managed to continue offensive operations in parts of both Syria and Iraq. Of equal concern, its beheading of foreign hostages appears to have created an element of leverage over the international community's ability to counter its influence.

The following chapters provide an in-depth profile of IS and its various predecessors—something that is lacking in contemporary open sources. They examine IS's history, evolution, current status, structure, military strategy, internal policy, and mode of governance. The book also explores

IS's future objectives and the policy options available to confront this new and growing threat in both the immediate and long term. Any strategy to counter IS must address the sociopolitical conditions in Iraq and Syria that the organization has engendered and exploited to fuel its growth.

1

"Lasting and Expanding"

OVER THE YEARS, members of IS and its various predecessor organizations have frequently been heard proclaiming *baqiya wa tatamadad,* or "lasting and expanding." This slogan concisely sums up the fundamental modus operandi of the IS organization, the roots of which date back to at least 1999, when its notorious father figure, Ahmad Fadl al-Nazal al-Khalayleh (Abu Musab al-Zarqawi) was released from prison in Jordan. Since then, IS and its predecessor factions have by and large met this simple objective, despite military challenges by the U.S.-led invasions and occupations of Afghanistan and Iraq.

1999–2003: FROM JORDAN TO AFGHANISTAN

Zarqawi was released from Jordan's al-Sawwaqa prison after serving five years of a fifteen-year sentence for weapons possession and membership in the Bayat al-Imam—a militant organization founded in 1992 by the infamous Jordanian jihadi ideologue Issam Muhammad Tahir al-Barqawi (Abu Muhammad al-Maqdisi). Shortly after his release, Zarqawi moved to Afghanistan, arriving in Kandahar Province with a letter of *tazkiyya* (a personal recommendation or reference) from then-London-based Abu Qatada al-Filistini, an alleged al-Qaeda operative.[1] Upon making contact with al-Qaeda's leadership, Zarqawi acquired permission and a $200,000 loan to establish a training camp.[2] He used this camp as a base for building his own newly formed jihadi group, Jund al-Sham.[3] Within months, the group was renamed Jama'at al-Tawhid wa' al-Jihad (JTWJ).

Primarily consisting of Palestinians and Jordanians, JTWJ quickly attracted international attention for its December 1999 plot to attack Amman's Radisson Hotel and at least two other popular tourist sites.[4] The foiling of this "Millennium Plot" by Jordan's General Intelligence Directorate forced JTWJ underground until the U.S.-led invasion of Afghanistan following the 9/11 attacks. Zarqawi's JTWJ then emerged to fight alongside al-Qaeda and Taliban forces, eventually fleeing to Iran in December 2001.[5] There Zarqawi's followers were provided housing and given other assistance by elements linked to the Afghani militant group Hizb-e-Islami Gulbuddin. Shortly thereafter, Zarqawi's cadre relocated to northern Iraq with the help of locally based Ansar al-Islam.[6]

2003–04: INITIATING IRAQ'S INSURGENCY

By the time U.S. forces invaded Iraq in March 2003, Zarqawi had established a small JTWJ base in Biyara in the Kurdish province of Sulaymaniya—which was targeted in the opening rounds of the U.S.-led air campaign in March.[7] This proved to be Zarqawi's initiation into a conflict that would come to define him and his fledgling militant organization.

JTWJ revealed its strategic intent in August 2003 with three significant attacks. The first took place on August 7, when the group detonated a car bomb outside Jordan's embassy in Baghdad, killing seventeen people. The second, on August 19, was a suicide car bombing outside the UN Assistance Mission in Iraq that killed twenty-two people, including the UN Special Representative in Iraq. Last, on August 29, the group targeted the Shi'ite Imam Ali Mosque in Najaf with another suicide car bomb, killing ninety-five people, including Ayatollah Muhammad Baqir al-Hakim, the spiritual leader of the Supreme Council of the Islamic Revolution in Iraq (SCIRI).

Naturally, JTWJ targeted U.S.-led coalition forces, but other attacks focused on Zarqawi's traditional enemies of Jordan and the Shia, whom Zarqawi viewed as the chief threats is to Sunni power in Iraq and the wider region. This three-pronged targeting strategy represented the path to Zarqawi's ultimate objective: to undermine occupying forces while simultaneously sparking a sectarian conflict in Iraq. Zarqawi believed his organization could take advantage of the resulting chaos to cast itself as the defender of the Sunni community and to usher in the establishment of an Islamic state.

While partly influenced by the unique power politics of Iraq, the sectarian element of this objective was of particular personal importance to Zarqawi, as reflected in his writings. He consistently riddled his works with anti-Shia rhetoric, often mined from the words of historical Islamic ideologues. For example, he frequently quoted Ibn Taymiyya's well-known warning: "They are the enemy; beware of them; fight them, oh God, they lie."[8] In fact, in his final public address before his death on June 7, 2006, Zarqawi exclaimed, "The Muslims will have no victory or superiority over the aggressive infidels such as the Jews and the Christians until there is a total annihilation of those under them, such as the apostate agents headed by the *rafida*"—a derogatory reference to Shia Muslims.[9] Zarqawi demonstrated his personal commitment to targeting the Shia and sparking sectarian conflict early on by authorizing his second wife's father—a veteran of the group's Afghanistan days—to carry out the Imam Ali Mosque bombing.[10]

2004–06: IRAQ CONSOLIDATION, AL-QAEDA TENSIONS

JTWJ ramped up its operations from 2004 through 2006, adopting the use of multiple suicide bombers in mass casualty attacks. To an increasing extent, Zarqawi himself was feared for the kidnapping and beheading of foreign hostages, beginning with American businessman Nicholas Berg in May 2004. Because of its prominence and extensive international recruitment networks, JTWJ became the center of a growing jihadi umbrella in Iraq, incorporating other similarly minded groups. In September 2004, after eight months of negotiations, Zarqawi pledged allegiance to al-Qaeda and Osama bin Laden.[11] From that point onward, JTWJ was known as Tanzim Qa'idat al-Jihad fi Bilad al-Rafidayn, often simplified to al-Qaeda in Iraq (AQI).

However, Zarqawi's relationship with al-Qaeda was fraught with tension, particularly because of AQI's brutality and mass targeting of Shia civilians, a fundamental point of difference between Zarqawi and his masters in Afghanistan and Pakistan. Whereas Zarqawi thought society across the traditionally Islamic world had been corrupted and needed cleansing through terrifying violence, al-Qaeda had dedicated itself to combating "apostate" regimes and avoiding, where possible, tarnishing the image of the jihadi project. This was famously revealed in letters from al-Qaeda leaders Ayman al-Zawahiri and Jamal Ibrahim Ashtiwi al-Misrati (Atiya Abd al-Rahman al-Libi) to Zarqawi in 2005.[12] Instead of pursuing fast results through dramatic and unforgiving brutality in the AQI manner, al-Qaeda, at least in the aftermath of the U.S. invasions, had called for a more patient strategy. At the same time, Zawahiri's 2005 letter did encourage AQI to prepare to establish an Islamic state in Iraq.[13]

AQI's sustained prominence continued to attract the support—whether ideological or pragmatic—of other Iraq-based insurgent groups. On January 15, 2006, AQI announced its merger with five other groups (Jaysh al-Ta'ifa al-Mansura, Saraya 'Ansar al-Tawhid, Saraya al-Jihad al-Islami, Saraya al-Ghuraba, and Kataib al-Ahwal) to form Majlis Shura al-Mujahideen (MSM), whose aim was to unite and better coordinate Iraq's jihadi insurgency. Zarqawi's death (along with that of his spiritual adviser, Sheikh Abd al-Rahman) in Baqubah on June 7, 2006, might have been perceived as a potentially fatal blow to the fledgling MSM, but it actually encouraged a strengthening of the organization. Within five days, AQI appointed Abu Hamza al-Muhajir (Abu Ayyub al-Masri) as its new leader, and four months later the MSM announced the establishment of al-Dawla al-Islamiya fi Iraq, or the Islamic

State in Iraq (ISI), with a fully structured cabinet. Then on November 10, Masri pledged *bay'a* (allegiance) to ISI leader Hamid Dawud Muhammad Khalil al-Zawi (Abu Omar al-Baghdadi).

Although it took years for the significance of these events to become clear, Masri's pledge of allegiance to ISI combined with the lack of any formal ISI pledge of allegiance to al-Qaeda catalyzed a gradual divorce between the two entities. Through the late 2000s, al-Qaeda remained determined that ISI remain its subordinate, ordering it to attack specific targets, but by 2010–11, the relationship had eroded significantly.[14]

2007–09: GOVERNANCE FAILURE AND THE SAHWA

The establishment of ISI was intended to represent a qualitative evolution whereby an insurgent group transformed into a military-political actor responsible for governing territory. By late 2006, it had reached financial self-sufficiency, raising $70 million to $200 million a year through a combination of ransoms, extortion, and oil smuggling.[15] However, as had been the case with AQI, ISI proved unwilling to compromise its absolutist ideology. Where it attempted to govern, this meant communities more often than not responded by opposing its presence. Put simply, ISI overestimated its capacity to engender Sunni support and overstretched its forces, leaving them vulnerable to what was coming.

By early 2007, locally formed tribal *Sahwa* (Awakening) councils had begun actively combating ISI territorial control in Sunni areas of Iraq, particularly Anbar Province. Backed by U.S. and local security forces, these Sahwa militias—with their extensive local knowledge—proved effective at counterinsurgency. This shift in dynamics shook up the status quo significantly, encouraging ISI to lash out against rival Sunni insurgent groups and minority communities seeking to rid themselves of Sunni influence. This latter point was demonstrated on an extraordinary scale on August 14, 2007, when four ISI car-bomb attacks against Yazidi villages in northern Iraq killed nearly 800 people.[16]

Although ISI succeeded in assassinating Sheikh Abd al-Sattar al-Rishawi, the leader of the Sahwa councils, on September 13, 2007, the group came under extreme pressure in Iraq within a few months, owing in particular to the proliferation of its enemies. Consequently, many of its foreign fighters began leaving the country, and sectarian violence decreased measurably.[17] Indeed, the perceived threat from ISI diminished to such an extent that the United States lowered the reward for information leading to the capture or death of Masri from $1 million to $100,000 in May 2008, after reducing it from $5 million in 2007.[18]

Having operated as a model insurgent force in the mid-2000s, AQI, MSM, and ISI had initially been moderately successful, seizing territory and establishing localized mechanisms for governance. However, as such structures were by and large rejected by the surrounding populace, openings presented themselves for a traditional counterinsurgency strategy. Targeted intelligence-led strikes against ISI's various levels of leadership were complemented by a broader bottom-up fight, led by the Sahwa councils and backed by the U.S.-led coalition. Consequently, ISI suffered significantly during 2007–09.

2009–11: RESTRUCTURING AND RECOVERY

While pressure on ISI continued through 2011, Sahwa efforts were weakened by the initiation of U.S. military withdrawal from Iraq from June 2009 to August 2010. The resulting transfer of security responsibilities to Iraqi forces dramatically reduced the Sahwa councils' capabilities and boosted ISI's confidence and local recruitment. Nonetheless, the pressure drove ISI into rapid operational learning. Amid the pressure associated with the Sahwa further south, ISI began in early 2008—with impressive speed—extensive structural reforms whereby it began "devolving" back into a typical "terrorist" group.

One particularly significant decision was to shift ISI's headquarters to the northern city of Mosul, where existing Arab-Kurdish tensions could be exploited. Initially, everyday ISI management in Mosul was led by Abu Omar al-Baghdadi's deputy, Abu Qaswarah al-Maghribi. Following his death in October 2008, Maghribi was likely succeeded by Abu Muhammad al-Jowlani, the founder and current leader of Jabhat al-Nusra, now al-Qaeda's Syria-based affiliate.[19] The move to Mosul facilitated ISI's recentralization of leadership, with power focused around Baghdadi and two deputies. The national leadership thus directed provincial strategy but delegated responsibility for specific operational planning and an enhanced focus on income generation to provincial governors. This bureaucratic structure required tight discipline, something that was at the time even encouraged in public propaganda releases.

Throughout this period of quite substantial learning, ISI continued to exploit existing political and social divisions. With the U.S. military withdrawal under way, Sahwa militias were growing disenchanted with Nuri al-Maliki's Shia-led central government owing to its lack of support and neglect of wages. By mid-2010, ISI was offering larger salaries than the government's monthly $300 and was therefore recruiting more and more Sahwa members into its ranks.[20] By early 2010, ISI also sought to rebuild its senior leadership, as thirty-four of the group's forty-two most senior officials had been killed or captured in the late 2000s, with only some being adequately replaced. To address this shortfall, ISI began launching well-planned, large-scale assaults on prisons holding its leaders.

ISI also shifted strategy, initiating an information campaign reemphasizing the legitimacy of its Islamic state project. In particular, it stressed Abu Omar al-Baghdadi's alleged membership in the Quraysh tribe, which according to Islamic tradition will produce the next caliph. Although Baghdadi was killed along with AQI leader Abu Ayyub al-Masri on April 18, 2010, his replacement as ISI leader, Abu Bakr al-Baghdadi, is also allegedly a Qurayshi. Similarly, ISI at times compared its political and territorial influence with that of the Prophet Muhammad during his time in Medina, thereby claiming religious legitimacy.[21]

More practically, ISI accompanied this internal change with an escalation of attacks in many areas of Iraq, particularly Baghdad. During August–December 2009, ISI carried out three of the largest and most significant strikes on central Baghdad since 2003, killing at least 382 people. Although Iraq saw fewer such large-scale attacks in 2010, the frequency of multiple bombings began to increase, signaling a bottom-up revitalization of ISI's operational structure. Perhaps most crucially, ISI had become far more Iraqi.

This improved its social grounding and led it to design operations at the provincial and local levels with community dynamics in mind. Also ISI was now better able to acquire intelligence sources within the Iraqi security apparatus—something it has since exploited extensively. Nonetheless, the scale of ISI's leadership losses in 2010 meant its structure and operations remained in the realm of a "terrorist" organization, albeit one that was increasing its influence in a growing number of Sunni areas.

2011–14: SYRIA, IRAQ, AL-QAEDA, AND A CALIPHATE

While the eruption of the civil war in Syria and ISI's expansion of operations into that country undoubtedly energized the organization's base, its recovery and expansion were clearly well under way before 2011. In early 2011, with the Arab Spring in full flow, ISI continued the expansion and professionalization that it had begun in late 2009. It significantly escalated its military operations in Iraq, both geographically, incorporating southern Shi'ite areas and the Kurdish north, and in scale, carrying out twenty to thirty attacks in multiple provinces, often within the space of a single hour. On August 15, 2011, for example, suspected ISI militants carried out twenty-two seemingly coordinated bombings in Baghdad and twelve other locations across

Iraq.[22] These intense and wide-ranging attacks aimed not only to inflict material damage on the government but also to diminish the morale of Iraq's security forces.

In July 2012, ISI initiated a "Breaking the Walls" campaign with a principal objective being the freeing of its many imprisoned members and senior commanders. Over the following year, ISI launched eight major attacks on Iraqi prisons.[23] Early on, the September 2012 attack on Tikrit's Tasfirat prison liberated 47 senior ISI leaders from death row,[24] while the campaign's finale was an assault on Abu Ghraib prison on July 21, 2013, that enabled approximately 500 prisoners to escape.

ISI also placed increased emphasis on collecting and exploiting vast amounts of intelligence, which proved hugely valuable as leverage over local authorities. This gave the group extensive influence across much of Sunni Iraq, which was advanced further when what was then ISIS launched a second twelve-month plan, Operation Soldier's Harvest (July 2013–July 2014). This campaign primarily aimed to undermine the capacity and confidence of security forces through targeted attacks and intimidation. Practically speaking, it entailed a 150 percent increase in "close-quarters assassinations" of security personnel and threats directed at individual commanders, soldiers, and police; these targeted attacks included the bombing of their homes, drive-by shootings against their checkpoints and personal vehicles, and other similar acts.[25]

The three years since 2011 have been extremely consequential for ISI's dramatic evolution and growth into an organization capable of conquering and governing territory. Most significantly, ISI has expanded into Syria, exploiting that country's revolution and civil war.

ISI and its antecedents had maintained links in Syria since 2003, when recruitment networks, facilitated by Syrian intelligence, funneled fighters from the Arab world into Iraq through Syria. By 2007, according to the U.S. government, "85–90 percent" of foreign fighters in Iraq had come via Syria.[26] Therefore the emergence of a popular revolution in Syria in early 2011 attracted the attention of Abu Bakr al-Baghdadi, who sent his operations chief in Iraq's Ninawa Province, Abu Muhammad al-Jowlani, to Syria to establish an ISI front.[27]

Jowlani arrived in Syria's northeastern Hasakah Governorate in August 2011 and began connecting with local jihadi cells across the country in order to establish what would become Jabhat al-Nusra.[28] Many of these cells had been formed by individuals released in a series of amnesties granted by President Bashar Assad, notably Decree 61 of May 31, 2011.[29] Jabhat al-Nusra then emerged publicly on January 23, 2012, claiming responsibility for a December

23, 2011, suicide bombing in Damascus that killed at least forty people.[30]

In the following six months, Jabhat al-Nusra operated in Syria similarly to ISI but insisted it had no links to ISI or al-Qaeda. Although Jabhat al-Nusra's targets were primarily government-linked, civilians bore the brunt, making the group unpopular with the Syrian opposition. In late 2012, however, this dynamic began to change significantly. By this time Jabhat al-Nusra had become a sizable militant organization, numbering perhaps 2,000 members, with particularly effective deployments in Damascus and Deraa in the south and Idlib and Aleppo in the north.[31] This expansion allowed Jabhat al-Nusra to transform itself from a typical terrorist group into an insurgent force, especially in the north. By mid-January 2013, Jabhat al-Nusra had led the seizure of two major military facilities in northern Syria—the Hanano barracks in Aleppo in mid-September 2012 and the Taftanaz airbase in Idlib on January 11, 2013—and cemented its reputation as a valued member in the fight against the government. In fact, when the U.S. State Department designated Jabhat al-Nusra a terrorist organization on December 11, 2012, the theme of that week's Friday protests across Syria was "We are all Jabhat al-Nusra."[32]

This remarkable rise prompted Abu Bakr al-Baghdadi to attempt to reign in his increasingly independent Syrian subordinate. On April 9, 2013, Baghdadi confirmed in an audio statement that Jabhat al-Nusra was an offshoot of ISI and that henceforth it would be subsumed into the expanded Islamic State in Iraq and al-Sham (ISIS). Jowlani promptly rejected this edict, and despite several months of wrangling, Jabhat al-Nusra maintained its independence, leaving ISIS to gradually emerge as an autonomous component within the Syrian conflict. To assert itself, this new Syria-based ISIS force—initially composed largely of former Jabhat al-Nusra foreign fighters—began aggressively expanding across northern and eastern Syria. This quickly prompted opposition; while Jabhat al-Nusra had so far willingly shared power and governance, ISIS demanded complete control over society.

ISIS's July 2013 killing of a senior Free Syrian Army commander and member of the Western-backed Supreme Military Council in Latakia was the first sign of the inevitable. Six months later in January 2014, after many similar incidents, a coalition of moderate groups launched operations against ISIS across northern Syria, eventually forcing its withdrawal east toward Raqqa in March 2014. By that time, ISIS's refusal to submit to independent opposition courts and to al-Qaeda–appointed mediators had pushed Zawahiri to announce in February that "ISIS is not a branch of the al-Qaeda group, we have no organizational relationship with it, and the group is not responsible for its actions."[33] Despite such losses, from 2013 onward, ISIS's unrivaled information operations, exploitation of social media, and adroit balancing of operational intensity in Iraq and Syria brought a renewed energy toward its cause of controlling territory and establishing an Islamic state.

Although the emergence of an anti-ISIS front in northern Syria caused the group to lose considerable territory in early 2014, the setback was temporary. Having consolidated ISIS's capital in Raqqa, its forces in Iraq exploited conditions in the Sunni heartland of Anbar to march into Fallujah and parts of Ramadi in January 2014. This marked ISIS's renewed venture into overt territorial control in Iraq and set the stage for its gradual expansion in Anbar, particularly along the Syrian border. ISIS then began a concerted counterattack against opposition groups in Syria's eastern Deir Ezzor Governorate in April 2014, focused along the Euphrates and Khabur Rivers. At this point, ISIS's operations in Iraq and Syria were becoming increasingly interrelated, with funds, fighters, and weapons crossing borders more frequently. It was under this emerging reality that ISIS led the rapid seizure of Mosul on June 10, thereby inflaming the wider Sunni armed uprising across Iraq.

To underline their accomplishments and goals, as well as to attract a wider following, ISIS issued a series of coordinated media releases marking the start of Ramadan. The most significant of these was an audio recording, released on June 29 in five languages, that announced the establishment of the caliphate. On the same day the group published videos titled "Breaking the Borders" and "The End of Sykes-Picot" that showed the physical destruction of a land barrier demarcating the Syria-Iraq border and a militant touring a captured Iraqi border post adjacent to Syria. A July 1 audio statement in which Baghdadi celebrated the caliphate's creation was followed by a July 5 video of his first public appearance as "caliph."

While this dramatic and choreographed series appeared to attract considerable support among a new, younger generation of potential jihadis around the world, the declaration of a caliphate was an extremely bold move, particularly in view of its lack of Islamic legitimacy. According to Usama Hasan, a senior fellow at the Quilliam Foundation, part-time imam, and expert on Islam,

> An Islamist caliphate, by definition, covers the entire "Muslim World." . . . The hypothetical return of a Caliph in Islamic jurisprudence implies a large degree of Muslim unity, with these united Muslim masses willingly pledging allegiance to him. This is the fundamental mistake of [IS], a fatal flaw for their

theological credentials. They may have been entitled to declare an "Islamic emirate" (as the Taliban did in Afghanistan) or even an "Islamic state," just as Iran, Pakistan, Afghanistan, and Mauritania are '"Islamic republics." But to declare a caliphate for all Muslims when they rule over, at best, a few tens of millions Syrians and Iraqis out of a worldwide Muslim population of 1.2–1.5 billion, is to destroy any notion of Muslim representation or unity.[34]

2

The Emerging Islamic State

SINCE 1999, IS and its antecedents have consistently worked on creating the necessary conditions for establishing an Islamic state. Although the group's initial roots lie in Jordan and Afghanistan, the vast majority of its operational history relates to Iraq and now, increasingly, Syria.

After a first attempt at state building in Iraq in the mid-2000s, followed by further efforts across northern Syria in 2013, IS appeared closer in 2014 to achieving its ultimate objective, international strikes notwithstanding. The scale and geographic spread of its operations, the extent of its territorial control and influence, its improved policy of governance, its vast wealth and revenue capacity, the professionalism of its information operations, and its continued global recruitment will keep IS a serious threat to regional and international security for many years to come.

Developing and implementing any effective strategy to counter IS requires a detailed understanding of the organization itself. As a first step, IS should not be thought of as merely a terrorist group, but, in fact, as a qualitative evolution of the al-Qaeda model. Not only is its military strategy more professionally designed and implemented, but a practical model for social governance also exists and has proved surprisingly successful within unstable environments.

However, the long-term prospects for this "state" depend on IS sustaining and exploiting instability and maintaining steady and significant sources of income. It will also need its local adversaries to remain comparatively weak and divided. As an organization, IS has benefited significantly from its financial and structural independence, but this is also an existential weakness that can be exploited.

MILITARY STRATEGY

By October 2014, IS likely commanded as many as 31,000 fighters, but most important, it had accumulated considerable territorial control, backed by a number of weapons systems and vehicles.[1] Its weaponry included tanks, armored personnel carriers, field artillery, self-propelled howitzers, multiple-rocket launchers, an assortment of antitank guided missiles (ATGMs), antiaircraft guns, and a small number of man-portable air-defense systems. While U.S.-led airstrikes in Iraq and then Syria have contained IS and slowed its momentum, a considerable portion of IS weaponry, despite being targeted, remains in play or in concealed storage.

If the group can survive strikes, its weaponry and manpower will remain capable of offensive operations into the long term. However, this will also depend on IS operating as an organization of well-trained, ideologically motivated, and ruthless fighters rather than a rag-tag group of militiamen. In this respect, IS has long implemented policies aimed at professionalizing its members. The number of training camps appears to have increased since 2013, and the group's social media output indicates that IS has been operating such camps in most sizable municipalities under its control, both in Syria and Iraq.

According to a series of interviews with IS fighters between December 2013 and August 2014, all recruits are responsible for securing *tazkiyya* from an existing IS member before heading into Syria or Iraq. Upon arrival, recruits are brought to prearranged accommodations shared with other new members. A British IS fighter, "Abu Dujana," interviewed in January 2014 explained: "I had a contact in Syria who helped me cross illegally after I was rejected at the [Turkish] border crossing. When I crossed, I drove two hours through [ISIS] territory. Everything was tranquil and beautiful, and it seemed life was continuing as normal. [When I arrived] I was mainly with Syrians, but there were also Saudis, Tunisians, a handful of Brits and French."[2]

After a series of interviews—during which personal information is logged, passports copied, and financial donations accepted—new recruits have to undergo several weeks of religious and military training. Such training typically focuses on the use of pistols, assault rifles, rocket-propelled grenades, and sometimes mortars. At times, additional training is provided on more sophisticated weapons. Upon completion, new recruits are ordinarily assigned to guard duty for several weeks before being entrusted with frontline military duties.

IS military operations can be divided into two general categories. The first is mass casualty urban attacks, normally targeting Shia, Alawi Muslims, and other minority groups, often in civilian areas. These attacks, which have been more common in Iraq, are typical of a terrorist organization, managing small, covert, largely urban cells linked to a larger militant infrastructure capable of providing funding and equipment. These operations can continue amid favorable or unfavorable environments and are the key to sustaining offensive momentum against adversaries.

This crucial facet of IS's military strategy aims to spark or sustain sectarian conflict—to "provoke [the Shia] to radicalize, join Iranian-sponsored militias and commit similar atrocities against Sunnis."[3] Recognizing that many ordinary Sunnis find the Shia-led government in Iraq and the

Alawi-led one in Syria repressive, IS aims to present itself as the protector of true and pure Sunni ideals.

This sectarian intent has been clearly visible in Iraq, but in Syria the picture is more complex. The group's "terroristic" tactics there have also been directed against Sunni municipalities controlled by groups hostile to IS, as a combination of retribution and intimidation.

The other category of IS's military strategy can be described as a concerted campaign of attrition against military opponents' capabilities and morale. In Iraq, such operations have focused primarily on Sunni urban centers and transport routes within primarily Sunni regions, particularly Anbar and Ninawa Provinces. In Syria, this has centered on resource-rich regions in the northeast and east of the country, as well as in areas bordering Turkey and Iraq, but mainly targeted opposition groups until mid-2014, when government targets assumed a heightened importance. Such activities require a more favorable environment—containing, for example, potentially supportive populations, a lack of capable adversaries, and ease of access to continuous resource supply—in which shaping operations can create the conditions necessary for acquiring and consolidating territory.

Before seizing Mosul, for example, IS spent several years of extensive intelligence-led operations on eroding the Iraqi security forces' capacity to control the city's periphery—particularly by repeatedly attacking checkpoints and patrols. Simultaneously, IS forces carried out a covert campaign of intimidation targeting military and government officials, reinforced by assassinations of senior, experienced individuals. Crucially, this impaired the government's ability to effectively control the city, thus allowing IS to establish a shadow authority capable of exerting covert influence by day and sometimes almost overt control by night.[4] This, in and of itself, undermined the community's belief and trust in its government-appointed protectors. Thus by the time the final offensive on Mosul began in early June 2014, the military's capabilities and confidence had been so weakened that the city fell in a matter of twenty-four hours.

This strategy was the most influential factor facilitating IS successes in 2013–14, which increasingly took the form of assaults conducted by light infantry units. Much of the responsibility for building up this military capability can be attributed to Baghdadi's former deputy, Haji Bakr (killed in Syria in February 2014), who purged the organization of most of its non-Iraqi senior leadership, replacing it with experienced former Ba'thist security officers.[5]

Specifically when assaulting large and better-defended targets, IS has typically launched multiple attacks on several axes, thereby overwhelming its opponent's capacity to defend. In the capture of Jalula in Iraq on August 11, 2014, for example, the group used two large suicide car bombs followed by twelve separate suicide bombers, all of whom attacked separate checkpoints across the town on foot, opening routes for several coordinated ground assaults.[6]

A different tactic was employed in IS's successful offensive in Syria's Deir Ezzor Governorate over April–July 2014. Having been forcefully expelled by opposition groups in February–March 2014, IS initiated a kidnapping and assassination campaign targeting local rebel leaders, complemented by several large car-bomb attacks against rebel command centers.

Roughly two months later, IS's dramatic offensive across Iraq and its establishment of a so-called caliphate precipitated a steady stream of rebel and tribal surrenders across Deir Ezzor. Each surrender strengthened IS's hand in other areas still held by rival opposition groups, which IS further weakened by offering peaceful surrenders in exchange for repentance and disarmament. Notwithstanding a rebellion by the Shai'tat tribe—which was brutally suppressed through the deaths of 700 men and the disappearance of 1,800 others—by mid-August IS had effectively consolidated control over much of Deir Ezzor Governorate.[7]

Independent of specific local dynamics, IS has proved capable of designing and implementing a multistage strategy aimed at engendering a chaotic power vacuum into which it can enter. By combining a typical insurgent strategy of attrition with extreme brutality (such as the execution of approximately 200 men captured at Tabaqa airbase in late August 2014), IS has acquired the leverage needed to become locally dominant. At that point, IS units can assume a central role in all local affairs. As Abu Usama, a British fighter based in Homs, explained in May 2014, "Our average day here is now normally much of the same—manning checkpoints, going on patrol in the area, settling disputes between locals and between tribes, and a lot of meetings with village elders and their chiefs, so we can discuss their concerns and complaints."[8]

But IS operates in complex environments. During its post–June 2014 offensive in Iraq, it has managed alliances with other armed Sunni factions, many of which it would ordinarily perceive as its enemies. While these "relationships of convenience" are far from steady—there have been frequent small-scale clashes, especially with the Ba'thist Jaysh Rijal al-Tariqa al-Naqshbandiyya (JRTN)—they will last while the greater fight against the government continues. In fact, despite tensions, JRTN leader, and former Iraqi vice president under Saddam Hussein, Izzat Ibrahim al-Douri clearly celebrated the lead role of "the heroes and knights of al-Qaeda and the Islamic State" in an audio statement released on July 13, 2014.[9]

To underline its investment in such alliances, IS handed out political appointments to two former generals in the Ba'thist Iraqi Army: Azhar al-Obeidi was named governor of Mosul shortly after the city was captured, and Ahmed Abd al-Rashid governor of Tikrit.[10] So far, its management of such relations has enabled IS to influence dynamics far beyond what its size would otherwise allow.

Despite widespread accusations that IS and the Syrian government have consciously coordinated operations, there has been no genuine evidence to substantiate such activity. It is indeed true that by the time a major anti-ISIS front emerged in January 2014, ISIS was no longer fighting government forces (and vice versa). However, a more logical explanation for that development is that both Assad and ISIS were facing more immediate adversaries at that point in time. Undoubtedly, Assad did have an interest in allowing ISIS to expand and have its influence divide and weaken the opposition, but the regime's immediate interests were focused further south—in Damascus, Homs, southern Aleppo, and the Qalamoun region. Meanwhile, ISIS interests were focused on the northeast, where its principal adversaries were opposition groups and the Kurdish Yekîneyên Parastina Gel (YPG).

IS's pragmatic balancing of interests shifted in July 2014 when, having consolidated control in Deir Ezzor and

Raqqa, the group launched several major offensives against government forces in Aleppo (at Kweiris airbase), Homs (at the al-Shaer gas field), al-Hasakah (at Regiment 121 and the city), and Raqqa (Division 17, Brigade 93, Tabaqa airbase). Put simply, IS had maneuvered itself into a comfortable enough position to relaunch operations against the Syrian government, which, theologically, it considers on par with the devil.

INTERNAL POLICY

At its most basic level, IS is a "revolutionary actor" whose entire modus operandi is designed to "project a goal of radical political and social change."[11] For precisely this reason, IS operates as a tightly controlled and bureaucratic organization.

While maintaining a "cabinet" composed of "ministers," IS's top leadership has become smaller and more exclusive since Abu Bakr al-Baghdadi's accession in 2010. Baghdadi likely maintains a personal adviser or assistant (formerly Haji Bakr) and below him two immediate deputies (one for Syria, one for Iraq), an eight-man cabinet, and a military council of at most thirteen men.[12]

At the top, Baghdadi projects a crucial image of Islamic legitimacy, justified by his apparent Ph.D. in Islamic Studies from Baghdad's Islamic University and his history as an imam and preacher in Samarra. Though he is not a graduate of al-Azhar or Dar al-Ifta' al-Masriyyah, Baghdadi's clerical background puts him on a qualitatively higher religious level than Osama bin Laden or Ayman al-Zawahiri.

More significant, however, is the military and intelligence experience held by many of Baghdadi's senior leaders, which has brought a level of professionalism to IS's ability to operate as an efficient and capable organization. For example, both of Baghdadi's immediate deputies were former ranking officers in the Iraqi military. Abu Ali al-Anbari, the chief of Syria operations, was a major general in the Iraqi Army, and Fadl Ahmad Abdullah al-Hiyali (Abu Muslim al-Turkmani), the chief of operations in Iraq, was a lieutenant colonel in Iraqi Military Intelligence and a former officer in the Iraqi Special Forces.[13] Moreover, according to data seized from the safe-house of former IS General Military Council leader Adnan Ismail Najem Bilawi (Abu Abd al-Rahman al-Bilawi) in early June 2014, the group has maintained roughly 1,000 "medium- and top-level field commanders, who all have technical, military, and security experience."[14]

The decision to rebrand the MSM the ISI in 2006, and specifically treat it as a *dawla* (state), is symbolically crucial. By perceiving and presenting itself as a state, IS has sought to control and govern territory and maintained a cabinet of ministers responsible for a broad range of "ministries," incorporating military, civil, political, and financial duties.

According to a report on unpublished U.S. Department of Defense documents, ISI operated a complex and detail-oriented bureaucracy between 2005 and 2010, which, according to the author, is still largely in place:

> [ISI] cells [in 2010] were required to send up to 20% of their income from local enterprises—such as kidnapping ransoms and extortion rackets—to the next level of leadership. Higher-ranking commanders would examine the revenues and redistribute the funds to provincial or local subsidiaries that were in dire straits or needed additional money to conduct attacks. . . . Reallocation and payroll costs—compensation to members and the families of deceased members—were by far the largest expenses . . . accounting for as much as 56% of all payouts at certain points of time. . . . When it became apparent that the "apostates and Crusaders" were successfully enlisting tribal support against them . . . Islamic State commanders set up a new agency within the governing structure to woo back the leaders. Even these visits by members of the nascent "tribal committee" were recorded

by the bookkeepers who kept close track of the cash, Qurans and other gifts given to what they referred to as "VIPs" before writing reports to higher-ups about how receptive the tribes were to the overtures.[15]

At times, IS's military has appeared administratively akin to a nation-state's army, with units rotating between active frontline duty, days off in "liberated" areas, and other deployments "on base." As British fighter Abu Uthman al-Britani explained while deployed in Deir Ezzor in June 2014, "To be honest, it's like how you live life in the West, except you have a gun with you. . . . [What your duties are] can depend on where you are, but your main duty is *ribat* [frontline guard duty]. . . . You can travel if you wish as holiday is given to you—all you need is permission on paper."[16]

One aspect of IS's internal structure and policymaking mechanisms that has proven decisive in enabling expansion is its generation of income. IS has been almost entirely self-financed since at least 2005, and according to the U.S. Department of Defense database, external funding to AQI, MSM, and ISI between 2005 and 2010 amounted to no more than 5 percent of its total "income."[17]

After assuming ISI leadership in 2010, Baghdadi established a financial command council, and Mosul cemented its role as a principal source of income.[18] By 2014 a complex extortion network there was generating $12 million a month. Notwithstanding a potential increase in private financial support following IS's increased public prominence, the simultaneous expansion in income-earning capacity suggests that the group has continued to be financially self-sufficient.

While more sustainable, income earned through extortion pales in comparison with the underground sale of Syrian and Iraqi oil. Illicit oil sales are not new for IS—by 2010 the group was thought to have been "siphoning off a share of Iraq's oil wealth, opening gas stations in the north, smuggling oil and extorting money from industry contractors."[19] But by late August 2014, energy analysts estimated that the group was selling as much as 70,000 barrels of oil daily from Syria and Iraq (at $26–$35 a barrel of heavy crude oil and $60 a barrel of light crude) to internal black market customers and external buyers in Iraq, Lebanon, Turkey, and Kurdistan.[20] By these calculations, IS's daily income ranged from $1 million to $3 million, which over twelve months would have amounted to $365 million to $1.1 billion.[21] However, the targeting of IS-linked oil facilities in Syria by the international coalition since late September 2014 will have significantly eroded the likelihood of such a prospect.

IS's finances have relied heavily on oil and gas, but other resources are being exploited as well, including agriculture, cotton, water, and electricity. The group is also known to operate an efficient kidnap-for-ransom operation, with four foreign nationals—two young Italian women, a Dane, and a Japanese national—all confirmed kidnapped by IS in August 2014 alone.[22] Perhaps in the hope of securing ransom or prisoner exchanges for other captives, IS took this tactic to the extreme in late 2014 and early 2015 through the public execution of American, British, and Japanese nationals, which has proved a powerful weapon. Despite a French denial, unnamed NATO sources in Brussels, for example, have claimed that IS was paid $18 million in April 2014 in exchange for four French hostages.[23]

Even in areas not under its complete control, IS still maintains extortion networks and protection rackets. IS units have also allegedly stolen antiques and sold them onto the black market. One Iraqi intelligence official claimed the group had earned $36 million in early 2014 from the sale of 8,000-year-old relics from al-Nabk, north of Damascus.[24]

While IS fighters have long imposed shadow taxation (and extortion) within areas under their control or influence, the group has begun to introduce more official taxation systems since the proclamation of the caliphate. For example, a customs tax is now imposed on the trucking business on the main highways of western Iraq. It targets trucks transporting food and electronics from Syria and Jordan via

Iraq's al-Waleed and al-Tanif crossings. As of September 2014, rates were at $300 for a truck of foodstuffs and $400 for a load of electronic goods, with an occasional $800 flat rate for trucks in general. The system itself is surprisingly professional, as journalist Mitchell Prothero has observed: "Not only does IS offer protection from bandits, but its tax collectors also provide traders with paperwork that shows they've paid IS taxes as well as counterfeit government tax receipts that truckers can show to Iraqi Army checkpoints, which allow them to pass without further payments."[25] In addition to shielding IS from traditional financial counterterrorism measures, such independent financial capacities have also provided a source of social leverage, whether through incentives to encourage tribal loyalty or by funding food provision and fuel subsidies to encourage popular support. During its offensive in Deir Ezzor in May–June 2014, for example, IS "spread $2 million in the area to entice tribes and leaders to permit their presence," thereby securing several strategic surrenders and pledges of allegiance.[26]

IS's ability to present an image of wealth and success has strengthened its recruitment of new fighters locally as well as from abroad. As one moderate commander based in Aleppo, speaking on condition of anonymity, remarked in June 2014, "Syrians join ISIS for money, simply because they can afford to pay salaries."[27] An Islamic Front political official, who also requested anonymity, put it bluntly: "ISIS is definitely expanding—it has a lot of money and right now, Syrians are so poor. Money changes everything—people will turn to and support extremism out of desperation."[28]

COMMUNICATIONS STRATEGY: SOCIAL MEDIA SAVVY

Another important facet of IS's internal operations is its effective use of social media and exploitation of international media attention. Through a network of provincial-level media accounts and several central media departments, IS had significantly outperformed any other militant group on Twitter until August 2014, when its entire Twitter structure was removed, possibly after a request from the U.S. government.[29] After briefly transferring accounts onto an independent, more privacy-focused platform known as Diaspora, IS established a more stable presence on the Russian social networking site VKontakte. This, however, was eradicated in mid-September.[30]

IS's coordinated release of particularly significant content has proved capable of acquiring an impressively large viewership. For example, the hour-long "Salil al-Sawarim I" video, released by IS's Al-Furqan Media on March 17, 2014, was watched by 56,998 distinct YouTube accounts within twenty-four hours. Two months after its release date, the video was tweeted 32,313 times over a sixty-hour period—an average of 807.25 tweets an hour.[31]

IS has also operated several Android applications, including Fajr al-Basha'ir (Dawn of Good Tidings), which links to users' personal information and releases officially coordinated group content via their accounts. Fajr al-Basha'ir was particularly active during the capture of Mosul on June 9–10, 2014, during which one of its centrally coordinated tweets became the first search result under "Baghdad" on Twitter internationally.[32] IS-linked accounts even hijacked hashtags affiliated with the 2014 World Cup in June, adding tags such as #Brazil2014 and #WC2014 to their military media releases in order to appear on all related searches on social media using the same term.[33]

An increased focus on English-language production since April–May 2014 indicates a shift toward greater international promotion of the idea of living within IS's new "Islamic State." The *Dabiq* magazine—slickly designed and published in English—has incorporated subtle mechanisms to broaden IS's recruitment base. A focus on Millah Ibrahim (the Path of Ibrahim, or Abraham) in *Dabiq*'s first edition, for example, was likely intended to remind readers of a well-known paper by Abu Muhammad al-Maqdisi attacking the Saudi royal family's legitimacy. Opposing the Saudi monarchy is the founding principle of al-Qaeda's

most powerful affiliate, al-Qaeda in the Arabian Peninsula (AQAP), so this focus could well have been intended
to attract AQAP supporters toward IS.[34] In fact, by mid-
August U.S. intelligence had detected "groups of fighters"
defecting from AQAP and the North Africa–based al-Qaeda
in the Islamic Maghreb (AQIM) to join IS.[35]

Social media have not only attracted recruits and worldwide attention but also enabled potential recruits to coordinate their arrival in Syria or Iraq, and to secure *tazkiyya*. IS's
coordinated network of interlinked social media accounts
has in addition allowed the group to maintain consistent
messaging in multiple languages. Note, too, that the group's
bitter battle with al-Qaeda was played out online.

GOVERNING THE ISLAMIC STATE

By declaring statehood for IS and the restoration of the
caliphate, Abu Bakr al-Baghdadi made the ability to rule
and govern the determinant of the organization's success. As
a result, IS faces what has been "a fundamental dilemma"
for jihadis: "They cannot attain their goals if they don't
govern, yet the record shows them repeatedly failing at
governance efforts."[36] Thus far, though, IS has maintained
control of territory, including multiple urban centers, and
its religio-political project has managed not only to sustain

governance but also to expand it. Local citizens living under IS rule have described its local administration as "fast and efficient" with "everything . . . coordinated [and all] parts of the administration are linked, [they] share information and in general seem good at working together."[37]

In Iraq, the group has benefited from being able to exploit widespread Sunni discontent with Shia-led governments perceived as being repressive to Sunni rights. A popular desire for a workable and stable form of Sunni governance has provided IS with a vacuum to fill. It is doing so with a combination of municipal administration (police, Islamic outreach, engagement in tribal affairs, recruitment and training, education, sharia courts) and aid-based services (humanitarian assistance and facility management). Thus IS has offered civilians much of what nation-state systems do, but with more intense oversight.

Mosul has exemplified this reality. Having taken a mere twenty-four to thirty-six hours to capture the city on June 9–10, IS hastened to release its *wathiqat al-madina* (charter of the city) on June 12, which in sixteen points outlined the new law of the land.[38] The regulations imposed in Mosul were modeled on what was already in place in Raqqa, where it took IS five months to subvert the authority of rival groups and take unilateral control in October 2013. At that point, IS began implementing its vision of governance, which, within a Syrian context of intractable civil conflict, subsequently led to relative stability and tacit popular acceptance.

The immediate period after assuming control over populations has proved the most crucial for IS. Bold shows of military power in the opening hours of capturing territory have enforced a perception of authority, which has consistently served to encourage mass surrenders of armed men in makeshift "repentance offices" set up by IS.

The implementation of a strict form of sharia law is clearly central to IS's governance. Among its rules, IS imposes the *hudud* (fixed Islamic punishments for serious crimes); enforces attendance of the five daily prayers; bans drugs, alcohol, and tobacco; controls personal appearance, including clothing; forbids gambling, non-Islamic music, and gender mixing; and orders the destruction of religious shrines.

The imposition of the *dhimmi* (protection) pact upon monotheistic non-Muslims has appeared in Raqqa (from late February 2014) and Mosul (from July 17, 2014). This has placed non-Muslims in a relationship of "protection" under IS, so long as they regularly pay *jizya* (a poll tax) and abide by several other strict regulations: most notably, they must not build additional places of worship, must remove all visible signs of faith, not bear arms, and not sell or consume pork and alcohol.[39] In practice, however, this "protection" has represented a demotion to second-class citizenship. In Mosul, the *dhimmi* pact has been accompanied by the threat of "nothing but the sword" if non-Muslims fail to agree, fail to convert to Islam, or fail to flee the city within forty-eight hours.[40] Property owned by Christians and Shia members of the Shabak and Turkmen communities was subsequently painted with the Arabic letters *noon,* indicating *nasrani* (Christian), and *ra,* for *rafida.* Within three days, the vast majority of the city's Christians and Shia had fled.[41]

As for members of non-monotheistic faiths, their treatment has proved utterly uncompromising. After several months of largely uncorroborated allegations, IS admitted in October 2014 that it labeled Yazidis *mushrik* (polytheists) and thus Satanists who could be legitimately enslaved and whose women could be made IS concubines.[42]

Ultimately, IS's political project is geared to establishing a *Sunni* Islamic state. Therefore non-Sunnis receive minimal rights, if any.

Because of its unstable surroundings, IS seeks to establish law and order immediately after capturing territory. Police forces—male and female—are rapidly formed and deployed to patrol the streets and enforce traditional civil and sharia laws, and sharia courts are promptly established. The speed of such mobilization is often facilitated by generous salaries. Despite this clear focus on law and order, the level of enforcement appears to differ in each locale. As of mid-October 2014, for example, the scope of IS's behavioral code in Mosul has not compared with the level imposed in Raqqa. Clearly, IS adapts to the unique dynamics it faces in different locations. In one respect, however, the group is consistent: the longer it is in control of a municipality, the more hardline and confident its rule becomes. Still, nowhere has this reached the level of extremity seen in 2008 when ISI banned women from purchasing sexually suggestive cucumbers and prohibited the sale of ice cream because it did not exist during the time of the Prophet Muhammad.[43]

IS does not just focus on disciplinary justice, however. It also spends significant financial resources on providing social services. One of its first steps upon capturing a municipality is to take control of industries and municipal services and facilities so as to ensure what it considers a more efficient and egalitarian provision of services. Consistently, this has meant assuming authority over electricity, water, and gas supplies, local factories, and even bakeries—all of which lend IS total control over the core needs of a civilian population.

Similarly, IS frequently subsidizes the prices of staple products, particularly bread, and has been known to cap rent prices. After assuming control of much of Deir Ezzor

Governorate in July 2014, for instance, IS funded the reduction of bread prices from 200 to 45 Syrian pounds and also made it mandatory for bakeries to provide *zakat* (a charitable obligation in Islam) to the poor.[44] In Mosul, IS established a free hospital the day before capturing the city and later capped monthly rent prices at a more affordable US$85.[45]

Civilian bus services are frequently established and normally offered for free. Electricity lines, roads, sidewalks, and other critical infrastructure are repaired; postal services are created; free healthcare and vaccinations are provided for children; soup kitchens are established for the poor; construction projects are offered loans; and Islam-oriented schools are opened for boys and girls. In Raqqa, IS even operates a consumer-protection office, which has closed shops for selling poor-quality products.[46] Put simply, IS attempts to provide the same services that a nation-state offers its citizens, but, according to the group, in a more ethical manner.

Religious education and proselytizing is another key element of IS's religio-political governance. In addition to introducing new academic curriculums, the organization frequently holds public *da'wa* (proselytizing) events to "educate" its constituents on the benefits of living under IS rule.[47] Children often receive free meals and gifts on these occasions and at times are also used to celebrate the pledging of *bay'a* by local tribal leaders or other dignitaries. According to IS fighter Abu Dujana, "When ISIS entered Homs Governorate, the people were very scared of us, but after four or five months, the majority of village chiefs had pledged allegiance to us and hundreds of their men had volunteered to join our ranks. . . . We had educated the people, taught them how to read, run vaccination clinics for children, stopped bandits and highwaymen, and allowed trade to resume properly."[48]

IS has devised a near-complete mode of governance, which, when combined with the organization's extensive financial resources, has by and large kept cities running and people tacitly content. When introduced in a broader context of conflict and instability, such governance finds Sunni civilians more likely to accept the imposition of its harsh norms. This factor is key to IS's survival or demise.

Executions—sometimes by crucifixion and stoning—and the amputation of limbs as punishment for murder, adultery, and robbery have demonstrated a shocking level of brutality. This "stick" combined with the "carrot" offered by social services has occasionally made IS appear, at least in the immediate term, to be a viable alternative to perceived repressive, sectarian, and foreign-influenced governments, on the one hand, and incapable, "moderate" oppositions, on the other.

3

Degrading and Destroying the Islamic State

IN THE WORDS of Brett McGurk, then U.S. State Department deputy assistant secretary for Iraq and Iran, the Islamic State is "worse than al-Qaeda" and "is no longer a terrorist organization . . . it is a full-blown army."[1] Indeed, as has been outlined throughout this book, IS is now in possession of a great deal of weaponry, operates like a tight military organization filled with dedicated recruits, and has proved capable of fighting as a light infantry force backed by heavy weapons. It has expanded considerably in recent years through a deliberate and methodical strategy of stoking sectarian conflict, exploiting political weakness, and exerting efficient and brutal military power.

Although its fundamental structure will always be that of a terrorist organization, IS has advanced beyond that in both its size and objectives, to a point where it is effectively building and defending a proto-state across Syria and Iraq. From a military point of view, it is like a Maoist-style guerrilla organization that melts into populations. Therefore IS should be treated as something qualitatively more significant than a terrorist organization, but with a significant counterterrorism component in any suitable strategy for thwarting it.

IS's expansion in Iraq and Syria has benefited greatly from tremendous regional instability and the weakening of nation-state borders. By exploiting and exacerbating such conditions, IS was able to gain military power, a multiplying international membership, and unprecedented financial resources.

IS's predecessor organizations survived the might of the U.S. military and a well-resourced tribal-based uprising, and today the sociopolitical conditions it faces are profoundly more favorable. The organization's five-step development—*hijra* (migration), *jama'a* (congregation), destabilization of *taghut* (tyrants), *tamkin* (consolidation), and *khilafa* (establishment of the caliphate)—has now been completed.[2] The most significant challenge that remains is to successfully consolidate and govern what could now amount to a proto-state without falling victim to its own ideology.

This challenge has been doubled by international military intervention, thus far in the form of air and cruise missile strikes. Operationally, this has come to represent more of a containment strategy rather than one dedicated to destroying IS power and territorial control. However, IS has lost some control in parts of northern Iraq and south of Baghdad, while external intervention has by and large checked IS's offensive operations and has forced the organization underground in areas under its control or influence.

The key to IS's future success and recruiting thus lies in its ability to sustain military momentum in the face of the containment strategy. Perhaps in the organization's favor, indigenous forces in both Iraq and Syria have proved largely incapable of launching serious counteroffensives that can capitalize on international strikes. If this situation continues, IS may well try to shift to a strategy of consolidation.

OBJECTIVES: IRAQ AND SYRIA

In Iraq, IS will likely continue the effort to destabilize social dynamics and to enforce a perception within the Sunni community that Haider al-Abadi's new government does not represent the population's rights. In Iraq in particular, the organization is deeply dependent on fueling instability and conflict in order to maintain its various marriages of convenience with other Sunni factions, without which it would struggle to maintain sufficient legitimacy.

Militarily, IS will seek to consolidate its authority in Mosul but without antagonizing other politically minded factions, such as Jaysh Rijal al-Tariqa al-Naqshbandiyya (JRTN). A campaign of consolidating and expanding territorial control is also likely throughout Anbar Province, notably in Hit, Haditha, and Ramadi, and also in Ninawa and parts of Salah ad Din. Moreover, a concerted campaign of insurgent-type destabilization attacks and occasional large-scale bombings will likely continue to target security forces in Kirkuk and Diyala.

At the same time, IS will probably launch a propaganda campaign depicting international strikes as contrary to Sunni aspirations and akin to an indirect invasion of Iraq. Without genuine political progress in Baghdad, such perception management is more than feasible. IS is also likely to gradually expand its bombings and other attacks across the capital and try to spark a sectarian tit-for-tat dynamic with Shia militias, in order to neutralize any attempt at Sunni-Shia reconciliation within the central government.

In Syria, IS will want to consolidate its control both in its capital of Raqqa and in the rest of the governorate. Meanwhile, its offensive campaign in the northwestern, largely Kurdish governorate of Hasakah will continue pressing to unite the areas it controls in northwestern Iraq with northeastern Syria. This will increase clashes with the Yekîneyên Parastina Gel (YPG), which may begin to draw in assistance from Iraqi Kurdistan and place the United States in a position of needing to (directly or indirectly) support what is technically a wing of the terrorist-designated Partiya

Kerkerên Kurdistan (PKK)—as was demonstrated around Mount Sinjar in August 2014.[3]

Despite international strikes, IS will likely maintain momentum in its offensive operations in western Aleppo as well, particularly around municipalities similar to and including the Kurdish border town of Kobane (Ayn al-Arab) and the opposition-controlled Bab al-Salameh border-crossing with Turkey. As in Iraq, it will also attempt to portray international intervention as an act of aggression against civilians and to exploit anger within swathes of the Islamist opposition for recruitment purposes.

In order to expand its operations, particularly to the south, IS could make use of growing frustration within the Syrian opposition, particularly among those who had chosen to retain links to Western-backed structures in Jordan and Turkey. Within this context, which includes strikes also targeting the widely popular Jabhat al-Nusra and other international jihadi factions in northern Syria, defections to IS were immediately reported by opposition sources.[4]

REGIONAL OR INTERNATIONAL OBJECTIVES?

IS objectives are all too clear in the remarks of IS fighter Abu Omar, interviewed in June 2014: "We are getting stronger every day in Sham and Iraq but it will not end there—of course, one day we'll defeat all the *taghut* regimes and bring back Islam to the whole region, including al-Quds [Jerusalem]."[5] IS's modus operandi in this regard is predicated on the expansion of its Islamic authority. However, the group does not yet appear to be in a rush to expand its operations. It has established a minimal operational presence in Lebanon, having claimed a suicide bombing that wounded eleven people in a Beirut hotel on June 25, 2014, and briefly capturing Arsal in the eastern Bekaa Valley during August 2–7 in cooperation with local Jabhat al-Nusra elements, which resulted in the death of twenty security personnel and the capture of nineteen others.[6] By early 2015, this presence will likely be fully established and active beyond border areas like Arsal.

In Jordan, IS maintains a small but strident support base in the southern city of Maan and areas within Zarqa, Irbid, and Salt. According to recent estimates, half of the approximately 2,000 Jordanians fighting in Syria and Iraq are IS members.[7] However, the Jordanian Salafi community's tendency to side with al-Qaeda, and thus Jabhat al-Nusra, represents a more notable threat to internal security, at least in the immediate term. The presence of multiple veteran jihadi ideologues—Abu Muhammad al-Maqdisi, Abu Qatada al-Filistini, Iyad al-Qunaybi, and Ayman al-Bilawi—in

Jordan in late September 2014 indicates the sheer clout that this pro–al-Qaeda community still possesses.[8]

Saudi Arabia has over 1,000 nationals fighting in Syria alone (mostly for IS) and almost certainly has an appreciable IS support base at home. The repeated appearance of pro-IS graffiti and leaflets and increasing terrorism arrests underline the heightening concern regarding the dangers posed by this apparent support base.[9] It is still likely, however, that al-Qaeda in the Arabian Peninsula (AQAP) retains more potential to carry out attacks on Saudi territory, although the significance of the proclamation of support for IS by senior AQAP leader Mamoun Hatem should not be ignored.[10]

Turkey has been widely blamed for the ease with which foreign fighters have been able to cross its border into Syria; it is also well known that IS maintains recruitment and facilitation networks in Ankara, Istanbul, and the southern border region.[11] Although the group was blamed for killing three people in Turkey's Niğde Province in March 2014, the value that such a seemingly permissive environment represents to IS makes it unlikely that the group will seek to expand operations into Turkey in the short term.[12] However, Turkish concerns that the large refugee population in the south could be used to establish a militant presence are rising. As Omer Faruk Cantenar, the chief of training at NATO's Center of Excellence-Defence against Terrorism explains, "Islamic radical terrorists are a big security concern for Turkey. . . . There are nearly 1 million refugees in Turkey and half of them are not in camps. This makes . . . it very difficult to have 100 percent control over the activities of those individuals."[13] Moreover, should Turkey more definitively crack down on IS facilitation and recruitment networks in Turkey, IS retaliation should not be discounted.

In North Africa, there is apparently a minimal pro-IS presence in the Libyan town of Derna, and rumors persist regarding the allegiances of Ansar al-Sharia in Tunisia and Ansar al-Sharia in Libya.[14] Pro-IS factions have begun to emerge in Algeria and Gaza, and the Egypt-based Jamaat Ansar Bayt al-Maqdis has begun acting in ways that suggest it is at least learning from IS's operational practices.[15]

Further afield, Nigeria-based Boko Haram leader Abubakar Shekau is said to have proclaimed in late August 2014 that the Gwoza Local Government Area of Borno State has become "part of the Islamic Caliphate."[16] At the same time, a splinter faction of Pakistan's Tehrik-e-Taliban Pakistan known as Jamaat-e-Ansar announced its support for IS, but remained at least officially loyal to al-Qaeda.[17] Meanwhile, in the Philippines the Bangsamoro Islamic Freedom

Fighters and a splinter faction of the Abu Sayyaf Group both announced their allegiance to IS.[18] In Indonesia, the imprisoned former Jamaah Islamiyya leader Abu Bakar Bashir pledged his allegiance to IS after allegedly facilitating the transfer of finances to the organization.[19]

Within the Levant or beyond, IS will want to develop a support base capable of provoking domestic instability before attempting to establish an actual operational presence. This process takes time, of course, making it unlikely that IS will do more than encourage localized instability in neighboring states in the coming months. However, should it succeed in consolidating its "state" in Syria and Iraq, it is quite possible that in 2015 it could choose to expand more directly.

FOREIGN FIGHTER BLOWBACK?

To judge by recent statistical studies, at least 15,000 foreign fighters from at least 90 countries are present in Syria and Iraq.[20] The unprecedented scale of this foreign-fighter flow has drawn a great deal of attention to the issue of "blowback"—or citizens returning to their home countries to carry out terrorist attacks.[21]

Some reports based on interviews with foreign fighters via social media have made light of the perceived threat of blowback, but foreign fighters operating public accounts online represent a very small portion of IS's manpower.[22] Moreover, those who have boldly claimed revenge for international airstrikes have expressed no desire to return home and instead seem resigned to being "martyred" in battle. As British IS fighter Abu Dujana explains:

> Before I left, I was just an average guy who wanted to help the oppressed. I wasn't a criminal and didn't have any issues with anyone or the police. But it wasn't difficult for me to [decide to come to Syria]. . . . It is a duty of all Muslims. . . . If we wanted to blow up buses, we could have learnt how to on the Internet and done so. Our objective is Assad, not Cameron. . . . We all have no intention of returning as we knew going to Syria was effectively revoking our citizenship. . . . Helping the oppressed is better than a red passport."[23]

Realistically, however, the chance that a foreign fighter might choose to return home to carry out an attack is quite unpredictable and should be treated as plausible. To judge by data from 1990–2010, approximately 11 percent of foreign fighters have become active security threats after returning home—not a small number.[24] For Western

Europe, which accounts for approximately 3,000 fighters in Syria, that would amount to 330 potential terrorists.[25]

Notably, three of the most recent and prominent terrorist attacks in the Western world involved native individuals with travel experience in foreign conflict zones—Syria, Dagestan, Kenya, and Somalia.[26] There is also the example of Syria-experienced fighters or individuals influenced by IS commanders returning to their home countries and plotting or successfully carrying out attacks. The cases of returning French nationals Mehdi Nemmouche and Ibrahim Boudina suggest the fears of such incidents are already being realized.[27]

Rising concerns have led European countries to intensify domestic security measures. In 2014 authorities in the United Kingdom, for example, carried out at least 500 percent more Syria-related terrorism arrests than in 2013, and on August 29 the British government raised the domestic terror threat level to its second highest. [28]

The threat of foreign-fighter blowback does not arise from IS-linked individuals alone. It looms large in other jihadi groups, particularly in Syria, which has become home to a considerable number of groups founded and commanded by, and containing, strong foreign-fighter components:

—Jaysh al-Muhajireen wa al-ʿAnsar, from Russia's North Caucasus (now a wing of Imarat Kavkaz)

—al-Qaeda

—Harakat Sham al-Islam, primarily from Morocco

—East Turkestan Islamic Movement, from China

—Katibat Suqur al-'Izz, primarily from Saudi Arabia

—Katibat al-Khadra', primarily from Saudi Arabia

—Jund al-Sham, primarily from Lebanon

—Junud al-Sham, primarily from Russia's North Caucasus

—Katibat al-Battar al-Libiya, primarily from Libya

—Usud al-Khilafa, primarily from Egypt

—Katibat Imam al-Bukhari, primarily from Uzbekistan

—Firqat al-Ghurabaa, primarily from France

—The De Basis and Sham al-Malahim networks, primarily from Belgium and the Netherlands.[29]

Many of these groups have expressed—directly or indirectly—an intention to continue operations within their home countries. In response, the United States on September 24, 2014, designated both Jaysh al-Muhajireen wa al-Ansar and Harakat Sham al-Islam terrorist organizations.

Individuals outside Syria and Iraq are equally likely to demonstrate their loyalty to IS by attempting attacks at home. The potential for such assaults has increased since September 22, 2014, when chief IS spokesman Abu Muhammad al-Adnani called on IS supporters around the world to attack citizens of countries involved in airstrikes against the group.[30] Even earlier, in mid-August, nineteen Malaysian jihadis linked to IS were arrested outside Kuala

Lumpur for plotting bomb attacks around the city.[31] The potential for such acts also became evident in Australia, in the September arrest of Onmarjan Azari for alleged terrorism plots and Abdul Numan Haider for an attack on antiterrorism investigators.[32]

IS presents itself as a superior alternative to al-Qaeda, particularly because of its success in controlling territory, governing populations, and posing a threat to both near and far enemies. So far, however, it has failed to eclipse its competition in directly attacking the "far enemy."

COUNTERING THE ISLAMIC STATE

A political official from Syria-based Alwiya al-Habib al-Mustafa has observed that "if the international community cannot live up to its values and promises to the Syrian opposition, then ISIS will be the only benefactor. Unfortunately, this is already happening and eventually, Syria will be worse than Afghanistan."[33] That likelihood increases by the day as IS continues to transform itself into an expansive, multilayered organization involved in military, religious, political, economic, and social affairs. By rendering much of the Iraq-Syria border irrelevant, IS has succeeded in destabilizing Iraq and creating conditions that have promoted disunity and paranoia within broad swathes of Syria's opposition.

To be effective, measures to counter IS's growth and eventually to defeat it altogether must treat it as more than a terrorist organization. A strategy of this nature must therefore incorporate not only counterterrorism practice but also aspects of economic, political, diplomatic, social, and religious policy. Because of this complexity, it will take a long time to counter IS and, crucially, will require local actors to take the lead, with the support of Western states, not vice versa.

An important step would be to accelerate and expand the existing policy of bolstering moderate opposition groups in Syria—through the provision of training, weaponry, and intelligence. The groups should be shaped around a more representative "national army" or a unified Hay'at al-Arkan (General Staff Command) based inside Syria. Only such a body would realistically have the potential to defeat IS.

Thus far Western policy toward Syria—notably the lack of measures to genuinely protect civilians from international strikes—has isolated much of the armed opposition. Within three days of the first strikes in Syria, the Western-backed Supreme Military Council and Western-supported Harakat Hazm, Jaysh al-Mujahideen, and Forqat 13, along with at least fifteen other major groups, had all condemned the intervention.

So long as Syrian military opposition groups do not receive what they perceive to be sufficient military and financial assistance, IS will benefit. Such assistance would aid in moderating Islamist and Salafi groups backed by the Gulf states, particularly members of the Islamic Front, and should be capitalized upon before the pendulum swings back. According to one Islamist fighter from Damascus, "If ISIS arrives in our areas, we will have two simple options: fight them or join them."[34] The latter possibility should not be ignored.

In tandem with such initiatives, increased efforts should be made to persuade Russia and Iran to suppress military assistance to the Syrian government and to recognize that long-term stability will be better served by ensuring a peaceful transition in Damascus. Iran's pivotal role in removing Maliki in Iraq is a model, albeit an insufficient one, that could be replicated in Syria so as to encourage a compromise political solution based on Assad's removal that would help counter the current instability and thus keep IS at bay.

In Iraq, existing contracts for military assistance to the government should be honored, but further assistance should be made strictly conditional. After the wholesale collapse of large parts of the Iraqi Army, particularly in June 2014, IS and other Sunni groups captured a significant quantity of Iraqi military equipment, much of it provided by the U.S. government. This collapse was emblematic of serious internal issues, and the continued provision of weaponry to such a body should be questioned without proven progress. To this end, Iraq should establish a significantly expanded program—to the one currently in existence—to monitor the rebuilding of the Iraqi armed forces and assess their capacity to counter IS over the long term. The influence of supporting Shia militias should also be reduced considerably. Relationships developed with Sunni tribes during the occupation of Iraq should be reconstituted and used as sources of leverage against IS. Over a longer period, a serious objective should be to initiate a second Sahwa or tribal-based "National Guard," although any such effort should avoid placing too much trust in diffuse and impulsive tribal forces.

Amid the collapse of government authority in northern Iraq, the Kurdish *peshmerga* has proved a more reliable force capable of confronting IS. It should be exploited for military and intelligence purposes. The significant expansion of the Irbil CIA station is a valuable step forward in this respect.[35]

In both Syria and Iraq, it is essential to develop and implement a broad strategy that explicitly aims to weaken IS's most significant strengths, specifically its revenue stream, the mobility of its forces, its effective leadership and command structure, its use of social media, and exploitation of ongoing regional instability.

The current approach to IS's revenue stream, which began in late September 2014, needs to be revised. Although much of the group's income is earned through the illicit production, refining, and sale of oil, the targeting of these resources themselves and resulting lack of supplies will have an adverse effect on civilian populations, especially in winter months. A wiser strategy would be to target the transportation infrastructure used to truck the oil to customers. This would have the added benefit of cutting off key nodes of IS communication and command and control. Steps should also be taken to expand and intensify existing international sanctions targeting those who may purchase or transfer IS-linked oil and other financial resources. Taken together, these would constitute an intelligence-heavy operation that would require local actors to play a substantial role, particularly in identifying targets and compounding IS losses.

An effective means of disrupting the mobility of IS manpower and resources would be to target its fleets of pick-up trucks and captured armored vehicles. IS is still a comparatively small military organization, commanding approximately 25,000–30,000 fighters in Syria and Iraq. Its consistent expansion depends upon continued military success, which by extension hinges on its mobility capacity. Crucially, this strategy should be carried out by local actors, backed by extensive air surveillance, airpower, and the provision of additional military training and equipment, particularly armor-piercing recoilless rifles and antitank guided missiles (ATGMs).

As for targeting leadership, the most effective measures here would stem from a concerted intelligence-led operation initiated at the local level by local actors. Their main objective would be to collect information on the identity and areas of operation of IS's senior leadership and military command structures. This intelligence should then be fed into existing military operations against IS, led by both international air assets and by local actors on the ground. A sustained erosion of IS's experienced leadership structure would make the group more vulnerable to military ground maneuvers by rival groups in Syria and, if established, in Iraq.

To counter IS's presence in the social media, aggressive efforts in this regard that began in mid-August 2014 with positive effect should be continued. Although permanently deleting all IS-affiliated accounts on social media would remove an extremely valuable source of intelligence—and is next to impossible anyway—the results of such consistent pressure would at least place IS on the backfoot and force it to devote resources to sustaining its online presence. At the same time, the organization's religio-political doctrine could be challenged and its motivations undermined through "mole" accounts—managed by government-paid individuals with extensive knowledge of Islamic creed and jurisprudence—placed within the online jihadi community. This measure could be doubly effective if the same sources were used to introduce divisions within the broader online jihadi community.

Because IS feeds off instability and perceptions of victimization, repression, and humiliation, it is essential to remove such conditions. If Iraq and Syria were to become stabilized, IS would soon find itself a fish out of water. In the case of Syria, the international community must recognize that President Assad does not represent a unifying leader for his country. Syria is a complex multisectarian and multiethnic state with a significant "middle ground," which so far remains relatively unengaged within the conflict. By replacing the binary image of opposition versus government with one that focuses on maintaining Syrian territorial integrity and social unity through national dialogue and engagement, the international community might encourage a peaceful solution in Syria. This would potentially be acceptable to Iran and Russia, but, crucially, will have to involve the eventual resignation or replacement of Assad.

In Iraq, political progress already under way in Baghdad should be built upon, and local Sunni actors, including those involved in armed activities, should be gradually engaged and drawn back into the national fold. The capacity of the government and its various structures to maintain a unified state whose constitution recognizes the equal rights of all communities must be reinforced. In this respect, Iraq is one very significant step ahead of Syria, but both states have far to go. Dedicated, long-term international support will be invaluable in sustaining such progress.

Much of this strategy will require an extensive program of intelligence collection and analysis incorporating human, geospatial, signals, open-source, and social media efforts. The conflicts in Syria and Iraq have revolutionized the use of open-source platforms for the release of material relating to insurgent and militant activities, thereby providing an extremely significant quantity of actionable intelligence. This avenue must be better exploited.

Perhaps the most significant aspect of this strategy is that it would greatly enhance the level of engagement with local actors. They hold the key to sustainably defeating extremism and laying the foundations for stable peace. In Iraq, this means assisting the recovery of the military, coordinating with the Kurds, and reengaging heavily with Sunni tribes. All three of these components have already been introduced, but they need to be substantially expanded both in scale and scope.

In Syria, the United States and its allies remain far too detached from the broader gamut of actors opposing the Assad regime, none of whom receive nearly enough assistance (finance, training, or equipment—lethal and nonlethal) to have a qualitative impact on the dynamics of the conflict there. Tribes, meanwhile, remain almost totally ignored, despite their significant potential to influence local society. One largely unengaged tribe, the Shai'tat, rose up against IS in Deir Ezzor in early August 2014 and spent approximately $6 million of credit over two weeks of fighting, before being brutally suppressed.[36] The Shai'tat received no assistance from the international community despite its very apparent determination to fight for the same cause.

On a multilateral level, security cooperation with regional states should be intensified, directed in particular at enhancing domestic counterterrorism, border control, and surveillance capabilities. The conflicts in Syria and Iraq have sparked sectarian and, in some cases, ethnic tensions throughout the Middle East, all of which are likely to remain for many years to come. Regional states must be better prepared for threats to their internal stability and security to prevent civil conflict spreading further.

It is equally important to recognize that the threat of foreign fighter blowback is realistic. The scale of foreign fighter recruitment into Syria and Iraq has been extensive enough to be an issue of high priority for Western intelligence agencies. Instead of maintaining a broad intelligence effort focused on preventing individuals from traveling *to* Syria and Iraq, a more efficient and effective approach would be to concentrate specifically on the (smaller number of) individuals traveling *back* to Western countries.

Since its initial emergence in 1999 in Jordan and Afghanistan, IS and its antecedent factions have evolved considerably, learning from experience and adapting to new operational environments. While it remains and has consistently been a terrorist organization at its core, IS has developed into a genuinely formidable militant adversary for nation-states both near and far. Militarily, IS has molded a professional and tightly organized senior and field command structure capable not only of planning, coordinating, and carrying out complex offensive and defensive operations but also of consolidating gains. Socio-politically, IS has established a model of governance that, despite its extremity, can be accepted on occasion by civilians living amid dire instability.

IS's principal weakness and potential source of its eventual demise, however, remains its uncontrollable determination to perceive its ultimate objective as global rather than local or regional. With the withdrawal of U.S. forces from Iraq, the eruption of civil conflict in Syria, and the proliferation of sectarian tensions across the region, IS was presented with near perfect conditions for its revival and strategic success. Its growth in Syria through 2013 and into 2014, its conquering of territory in Iraq's Anbar in January 2014, and its capture of Mosul in June 2014 all served to underline IS's very real prospects.

However, the kidnap and very public execution of American and British hostages in Syria beginning in August 2014 symbolized a strategic shift. Although the murders were initiated in retaliation or revenge for U.S. airstrikes in Iraq, they only served to heighten the likelihood of more intensive intervention. Moreover, IS's official directive in late September 2014 calling for its followers around the world to target Western nationals "wherever they may be" reinforced the then already emerging perception that IS represented a real international threat.

This is now a genuine reality. With external intervention in Iraq and Syria well under way, the only hope for neutralizing the danger that IS poses is to ameliorate existing

political failures in those countries and to bolster representative and popular local forces to combat IS militants on
the ground. In that sense, international actors must play
the vital role of facilitators, guarantors, and enforcers, but
it is the local players who will come to define the long-term
fate of IS.

Who's Who in the Islamic State Senior Leadership

THIS APPENDIX HAS been compiled using information gleaned from open sources and the author's personal research, which was concluded on October 20, 2014. The Islamic State is ordinarily very transparent regarding the death of members, including senior commanders, and it is therefore assumed these named individuals are still alive. However, since the initiation of international strikes in Iraq and Syria, the death of such individuals cannot be discounted. Moreover, the replacement of individuals is also distinctly possible.

A note about names: Jihadis rarely use the names given them at birth. The jihadi name is ordinarily a *kunya* (a name derived from the person's first child, that is, Abu Abdullah, or father of Abdullah), and this is the name that people would know the individual by. This is why I retain the jihadi name, rather than the birth name, throughout the text.

Caliph Ibrahim': **Abu Bakr al-Baghdadi**

Name at birth: Ibrahim Awwad Ibrahim Ali al-Badri al-Samarra'yy

An Iraqi national from the Al-Bu Badri tribe and an alleged descendant of the Prophet Muhammad. Received a Ph.D. in Islamic studies in Baghdad before founding Jamaat Jaish Ahl al-Sunnah wal Jamaa in 2003 to fight U.S. forces. Joined Majlis Shura al-Mujahideen (MSM) in 2006 and took charge of ISI sharia committees by 2007.

Source: Official Islamic State (IS) media content.

Deputy, Iraq: **Abu Muslim al-Turkmani**

Name at birth: Fadl Ahmad Abdullah al-Hiyali

A former lieutenant colonel in the Iraqi Army and a former officer in the Iraqi Special Forces. From Tel Afar, Ninawa. Allegedly killed in a coalition airstrike in late 2014.

Sources: Hisham al-Hashimi and Telegraph interactive team, "Revealed: The Islamic State 'Cabinet,' From Finance Minister to Suicide Bomb Deployer," *The Telegraph*, July 9, 2014; Julian E. Barnes, "Several Islamic State Leaders Have Been Killed in Iraq, U.S. Says," *Wall St. Journal*, December 18, 2014.

Deputy, Syria: **Abu Ali al-Anbari**

Name at birth: Unknown

A former major general in the Iraqi military from Anbar.

Source: Ruth Sherlock, "Inside the Leadership of the Islamic State: How the New 'Caliphate' Is Run," *The Telegraph*, July 9, 2014.

War Minister: **Abu Suleiman**

Name at birth: Nasser al-Din Allah Abu Suleiman

Source: Hanein Jihadist Forum, July 2, 2014.

Chief of Syria Military Operations: **Umar al-Shishani**

Name at birth: Tarkhan Tayumurazovich Batirashvili

An ethnic Chechen Georgian national. Former sergeant in Georgian military intelligence unit. Led Jaish al-Muhajireen wal Ansar in Syria before joining Islamic State in Iraq and Syria (ISIS).

Source: Official IS media content.

Senior Military Commander: **Abu Wahib**

Name at birth: Shaker Wahib al-Fahdawi

Arrested in 2006 by U.S. forces and sentenced to death. Escaped prison in Tikrit in September 2012.

Source: Official IS media content.

Chief Spokesman: **Abu Muhammad al-Adnani**

Name at birth: Taha Subhi Falaha

A Syrian national from Idlib who pledged allegiance to Abu Musab al-Zarqawi in 2002–03. Has been a military instructor and emir of Haditha and was imprisoned by American forces in mid-2000s.

Source: Official IS media content.

Minister of General Management: **Abu Abd al-Kadir**

Name at birth: Shawkat Hazm al-Farhat

Source: "Revealed: The Islamic State 'Cabinet,'" *The Telegraph*, July 9, 2014.

Minister of Prisoners: **Abu Mohammed**

Name at birth: Bashar Ismail al-Hamdani

Source: "Revealed: The Islamic State 'Cabinet,'" *The Telegraph*, July 9, 2014.

Minister of General Security: **Abu Louay/Abu Ali**

Name at birth: Abd al-Wahid Khadir Ahmad

Source: "Revealed: The Islamic State 'Cabinet,'" *The Telegraph*, July 9, 2014.

Minister of Finance: **Abu Salah**

Name at birth: Muafaq Mustafa Mohammed al-Karmoush

Source: "Revealed: The Islamic State 'Cabinet,'" *The Telegraph*, July 9, 2014.

Minister of General Coordination: **Abu Hajjar al-Assafi**

Name at birth: Mohammed Hamid al-Dulaimi

Responsible for coordinating communications and the distribution of resources within the Islamic State.

Source: "Revealed: The Islamic State 'Cabinet,'" *The Telegraph*, July 9, 2014.

Minister of Foreign Fighters and Suicide Bombers: **Abu Kassem**

Name at birth: Abdullah Ahmad al-Mashadani

Source: "Revealed: The Islamic State 'Cabinet,'" *The Telegraph*, July 9, 2014.

Minister for Social Services: **Abu Saji**

Name at birth: Aouf Abd al-Rahman al-Arfi

Minister for Weapons: **Abu Sima**

Name at birth: Faris Riyadh al-Nuaimi

Minister for Explosives: **Abu Kifah**

Name at birth: Khairy Abd al-Hamoud al-Taiy

Source: "Revealed: The Islamic State 'Cabinet,'" *The Telegraph,* July 9, 2014.

Governor of Baghdad: **Abu Maysara**

Name at birth: Ahmed Abd al-Kader al-Jazza

Source: "Revealed: The Islamic State 'Cabinet,'" *The Telegraph*, July 9, 2014.

Governor of Anbar: **Abu Abd al-Salem/Abu Mohammed al-Sweidawi**

Name at birth: Adnan Latif Hamid al-Sweidawi

Source: "Revealed: The Islamic State 'Cabinet,'" *The Telegraph*, July 9, 2014.

Governor of Salah ad Din: **Abu Nabil**

Name at birth: Wissam Abdu Zaid al-Zubaidi

Source: "Revealed: The Islamic State 'Cabinet,'" *The Telegraph*, July 9, 2014.

Governor of Kirkuk: **Abu Fatima**

Name at birth: Naima Abd al-Naif al-Jouburi

Source: "Revealed: The Islamic State 'Cabinet,'" *The Telegraph*, July 9 2014.

Governor of South and Central Euphrates: **Abu Fatima**

Name at birth: Ahmed Mohsen Khalal al-Juhayshi

Source: "Revealed: The Islamic State 'Cabinet,'" *The Telegraph*, July 9, 2014.

Governor of "Border Provinces": **Abu Jurnas**

Name at birth: Rathwan Talib Hussein Ismail al-Hamdani

Source: "Revealed: The Islamic State 'Cabinet,'" *The Telegraph*, July 9, 2014.

Governor of Ninawa: **Unknown**

Name at birth: Unknown

Governor of Raqqa: **Abu Luqman**

Name at birth: Ali Moussa al-Hawikh

A Syrian national released from prison during President Assad's amnesties in the summer of 2011.

Governor of Aleppo: **Abu Atheer al-Absi**

Name at birth: Unknown

Younger brother of Firas al-Absi (also known as Sheikh Abu Mohammed al-Absi), who was assassinated by Kataib al-Farouq in Syria in August 2012. Some reports claim Abu Atheer may have been redeployed elsewhere, possibly to Homs.

Governor of Deir ez Zour: **Haji Abd al-Nasser**
Name at birth: Unknown

Governor of Damascus: **Unknown**
Name at birth: Unknown

Governor of Homs: **Abu Shuayb al-Masri**
Name at birth: Unknown

Governor of Al-Barakah (Hasakah): **Abu Usama al-Iraqi**
Name at birth: Unknown

Senior Facilitator and Financier: **Abu Umar**

Name at birth: Tariq Bin al-Tahar Bin al-Falih al-Awni al-Harzi

A Tunisian senior facilitator responsible for the recruitment of foreign fighters and the collection of finance, based in Syria.

Chief of Media Operations: **Ahmad Abousamra** (name at birth)

A Syrian American national credited with managing ISIS's media operations, allegedly from Aleppo.

Source: FBI, *Most Wanted Terrorists*.

Senior Military Official: **Abu Ahmed al-Alwani**

Name at birth: Walid Jassim al-Alwani

A former Iraqi Army officer.

Sharia Official: **Abu Hummam al-Athari**

Name at birth: Turki al-Binali

A Bahraini national with Islamic training experience under Jordanian Abu Mohammed al-Maqdisi. Wrote first biography of Abu Bakr al-Baghdadi.

Source: Official IS media content.

Coordinator of Prisoners and Women's Affairs: **Abu Suja**

Name at birth: Abd al-Rahman al-Afari

Source: "Revealed: The Islamic State 'Cabinet,'" *The Telegraph*, July 9, 2014.

Senior Commander: **Abu Abdullah al-Kosofi**

Name at birth: Lavdrim Muhaxheri

A Kosovar Albanian ISIS commander, operational in both Syria and Iraq.

Source: Official IS media content.

Senior Commander: **Abu Khattab al-Kurdi**

Name at birth: Unknown

An Iraqi Kurd thought to have led the offensive on Kobane, Syria, in September and October 2014.

Source: Official IS media content.

Senior Commander: **Abu Jandal al-Masri**

Name at birth: Unknown

A senior Egyptian commander who led the siege and capture of Minnagh airbase in Aleppo in August 2013.

Source: Official IS media content.

Senior Commander: **Abu Huzaifa al-Yemeni**

Name at birth: Unknown

A prominent Yemeni commander with operational history in both Anbar, Iraq, and Raqqa, Syria.

Source: Official IS media content.

Explosives Expert: **Abu Omar al-Qirdash**

Name at birth: Unknown

An ethnic Turkmen and former Iraqi Army officer with militant command experience in Iraq, Syria, and Lebanon.

Senior Official: **Abu Omar "the boxer"**

Name at birth: Unknown

An Iraqi national who escaped prison in Tikrit in September 2012 and has since led operations in Idlib and Aleppo.

Senior official: **Abu Nasser al-Amni**

Name at birth: Mahmoud al-Khadir

A senior official in Raqqa. Extremely secretive, known for not uncovering his face and wearing gloves to cover skin tone.

Senior Official: **Abu Musab al-Hallous**

Name at birth: Khalaf al-Thiyabi Hallous

A Syrian national credited with managing ISIS's takeover of Raqqa in 2013.

Prominent Member: **Salim Benghalem** (name at birth)

A French national previously imprisoned in France in 2001 for murder. Allegedly responsible for executions in Syria.

Additional Sources

"Profile: The Rise of the Islamic State (IS)," TahrirSy, July 12, 2014 (http://tahrirsouri. com/2014/07/12/ profile-the-rise-of-the-islamic-state-is/).

U.S. Department of State, "State Dept. Designations of Foreign Terrorist Fighters," September 24, 2014 (http:// translations.state.gov/st/english/text-trans/2014/ 09/20140925308905.html#axzz3GmEGq8fh).

U.S. Department of the Treasury, "Treasury Designates Twelve Foreign Terrorist Fighter Facilitators," September 24, 2014 (www.treasury.gov/press-center/press-releases/Pages/ jl2651.aspx).

Notes

INTRODUCTION

1. Charles Lister, "ISIS: What Will the Militant Group Do Next?" *BBC News,* June 27, 2014 (www.bbc.com/news/world-middle-east-28053489).

2. Reports that ISIS seized $430 million from banks in Mosul have likely been debunked. See Borzou Daragahi, "Biggest Bank Robbery That 'Never Happened'—$400m ISIS Heist," *Financial Times,* June 17, 2014 (www.ft.com/intl/cms/s/0/0378d4f4-0c28-11e4-9080-00144 feabdc0.html#axzz380w59yNx).

3. Luay al-Khatteeb, "The UN Strikes Back at ISIL's Black Economy," *Huffington Post*, August 23, 2014 (www.huffingtonpost.com/luay-al-khatteeb/the-un-strikes-back-at-isil_b_5702240.html); Martin Chulov, "How an Arrest in Iraq Revealed ISIS' $2bn Jihadist Network," *The Guardian,* June 15, 2014 (www.theguardian.com/world/2014/jun/15/iraq-isis-arrest-jihadist-wealth-power).

CHAPTER 1

1. Bruce Riedel, *The Search for Al Qaeda: Its Leadership, Ideology, and Future* (Brookings, 2010), p. 94.

2. "Tracking Al Qaeda in Iraq's Zarqawi: Interview with Ex-CIA Analyst Nada Bakos," *Musings on Iraq* (blog), June 30, 2014 (http://musingsoniraq.blogspot.com/2014/06/tracking-al-qaeda-in-iraqs-zarqawi.html).

3. Riedel, *The Search for Al Qaeda*, p. 94.

4. Ibid., p. 96.

5. Loretta Napoleoni, *Insurgent Iraq: Al-Zarqawi and the New Generation* (New York: Seven Stories Press, 2005), pp. 104–05.

6. Saif al-Adel, "My Experience with Abu Musab al-Zarqawi," *Minbar al-Tawhid wa al-Jihad* (blog) (www.tawhed.ws/r?i=ttofom6f).

7. Nimrod Raphaeli, "The Sheikh of the Slaughterers: Abu Mus'ab al-Zarqawi and the Al-Qaeda Connection," Inquiry & Analysis Series Report 231 (Washington: The Middle East Media Research Institute, July 1, 2005) (www.memri.org/report/en/print1406.htm).

8. For example, see Zarqawi's letter to "the two honorable brothers," February 2004, U.S. Department of State Archive (http://20012009.state.gov/p/nea/rls/31694.htm).

9. Nibras Kazimi, "Zarqawi's Anti-Shia Legacy: Original or Borrowed?" Hudson Institute, November 1, 2006 (www.hudson.org/research/9908-zarqawi-s-anti-shia-legacy-original-or-borrowed-#BkMkToFoot2). The term *rafida* refers to the Shia, emphasizing their rejection of the first three caliphs following the Prophet Muhammad.

10. Zaki Chehab, *Inside the Resistance: Reporting from Iraq's Danger Zone* (New York: Nation Books, 2006), p. 47.

11. "Al-Jamaa Hassan Hussain li Ahl al-Islam," *Muskar al-Battar* 21 (2004) (http://ia600407.us.archive.org/6/items/AL-BATAR-Leaflet/021.pdf).

12. Zawahiri to Zarqawi, July 9, 2005, GlobalSecurity.org, (www.globalsecurity.org/security/library/report/2005/zawahiri-zarqawi-letter_9jul2005.htm); Libi to Zarqawi, Combating Terrorism Center at West Point, December 10, 2005 (www.ctc.usma.edu/wp-content/uploads/2013/10/Atiyahs-Letter-to-Zarqawi-Original.pdf).

13. Zawahiri to Zarqawi, July 9, 2005.

14. Will McCants, "State of Confusion: ISIS Strategy and How to Counter it," *Foreign Affairs*, September 10, 2014 (www.foreignaffairs.com/articles/141976/william-mccants/state-of-confusion).

15. Matthew Levitt, "Declaring an Islamic State, Running a Criminal Enterprise," *The Hill*, July 7, 2014 (http://thehill.com/blogs/pundits-blog/211298-declaring-an-islamic-state-running-a-criminal-enterprise).

16. "Yazidis in Iraq: A Tough Time," *The Economist*, November 13, 2013 (www.economist.com/blogs/pomegranate/2013/11/yazidis-iraq).

17. Colin Kahl, "Breaking Dawn: Building a Long-term Strategic Partnership with Iraq," *Foreign Policy*, August 31, 2010 (http://mideast africa.foreignpolicy.com/posts/2010/08/31/breaking_dawn).

18. Mike Mount, "Reward for Wanted Terrorist Drops," *CNN*, May 13, 2008 (http://edition.cnn.com/2008/WORLD/meast/05/13/pentagon.masri.value/).

19. "Al-Baghdadi Confirms the Death of Al-Qaeda in Iraq Second-in-Command," *CBS News*, October 23, 2008 (www.cbsnews.com/news/al-baghdadi-confirms-the-death-of-al-qaeda-in-iraqs-second-in-command/).

20. Timothy Williams and Duraid Adnan, "Sunnis in Iraq Allied with U.S. Rejoin Rebels," *New York Times*, October 16, 2010 (www.nytimes.com/2010/10/17/world/middleeast/17awakening.html?pagewanted=all&_r=0).

21. Brian Fishman, "Redefining the Islamic State: The Rise and Fall of Al-Qaeda in Iraq," National Security Studies Program Policy Paper (Washington: New America Foundation, August 2011) (http://security.newamerica.net/sites/newamerica.net/files/policydocs/Fishman_Al_Qaeda_In_Iraq.pdf).

22. "FACTBOX: Security Developments in Iraq, August 15," Reuters, August 15, 2011 (www.trust.org/item/?map=factbox-security-developments-in-iraq-august-15/).

23. Jessica D. Lewis, "Al-Qaeda in Iraq Resurgent: The Breaking the Walls Campaign, Part I," Middle East Security Report 14 (Washington: Institute for the Study of War, September 2013) (www.understanding war.org/sites/default/files/AQI-Resurgent-10Sept_0.pdf).

24. Tim Arango and Eric Schmitt, "Escaped Inmates from Iraq Fuel Syrian Insurgency," *New York Times*, February 12, 2014 (www.nytimes.com/2014/02/13/world/middleeast/escaped-inmates-from-iraq-fuel-syria-insurgency.html).

25. Michael Knights, "ISIL's Political-Military Power in Iraq," *CTC Sentinel*, August 27, 2014 (www.ctc.usma.edu/posts/isils-political-military-power-in-iraq).

26. Peter Neumann, "Suspects into Collaborators," *London Review of Books* 36 (April 3, 2014): 19–21.

27. Zeina Karam and Qassim Abdul-Zahra, "Al Qaeda's Nusra Front Leader Stays in Syria Shadows," Associated Press, November 4, 2013 (www.thenational.ae/world/middle-east/al-qaedas-nusra-front-leader-stays-in-syrias-shadows).

28. Rania Abouzeid, "The Jihad Next Door: The Syrian Roots of Iraq's Newest Civil War," *Politico*, June 23, 2014 (www.politico.com/magazine/story/2014/06/al-qaeda-iraq-syria-108214.html#.U9NsJVYpTRo).

29. Ibid.; interviews with several Syrian tribal sheikhs from Raqqa and Deir Ezzor by the author, August 2014.

30. "Declaration of Jabhat al-Nusra for the People of Syria from the Mujahideen of Syria in the Fields of Jihad," *al-Manarah al-Bayda Foundation for Media Production*, January 23, 2012 (http://jihadology.net/2012/01/24/al-manarah-al-bayda-foundation-for-media-production-presents-for-the-people-of-syria-from-the-mujahidin-of-syria-in-the-fields-of-jihad-jabhah-al-nusrah-the-front-of-victory); "Forty Killed, 100 Wounded in Damascus Blasts—TV," Reuters, December 23, 2011 (www.trust.org/item/?map=forty-killed-100-wounded-in-damascus-blasts--tv/).

31. Author's calculations.

32. "Syrians March in Support of Jabhat al-Nusra Militants," *France 24*, December 16, 2012 (www.france24.com/en/20121216-syria-march-support-jabhat-nusra-militants-us-terrorist/).

33. "On the Relationship of Al-Qaeda and the Islamic State in Iraq and al-Sham," *Al-Fajr Media*, February 4, 2014 (http://jihadology. net/2014/02/02/as-sahab-media-presents-a-new-statement-from-al-qaidah-on-the-relationship-of-qaidat-al-jihad-and-the-islamic-state-of-iraq-and-al-sham).

34. Usama Hasan, interview by the author, August 27, 2014.

CHAPTER 2

1. "Islamic State Fighter Estimate Triples—CIA," *BBC News*, September 12, 2014 (www.bbc.com/news/world-middle-east-29169914).

2. Abu Dujana, interview by the author, January 2014.

3. Aaron Zelin, "The Massacre Strategy: Why ISIS Brags about Its Brutal Sectarian Murders," *Politico*, June 17, 2014 (www.politico. com/magazine/story/2014/06/the-massacre-strategy-107954_full. html#.U6DqY41dUnY).

4. *Iraq at a Crossroads: Options for U.S. Policy, Before the Senate Foreign Relations Committee*, 113th Cong. (2014) (statement of Brett McGurk, deputy assistant secretary of state for Iraq and Iran) (www.foreign.senate.gov/imo/media/doc/McGurk%20Testimony%20 072414-Final%20Version%20REVISED.pdf).

5. Mitchell Prothero, "How 2 Shadowy ISIS Commanders Designed Their Iraq Campaign," *McClatchy DC*, June 30, 2014 (www.mcclatchydc. com/2014/06/30/231952/how-2-shadowy-isis-commanders.html).

6. Michael Knights, "ISIL's Political-Military Power in Iraq," *CTC Sentinel*, August 27, 2014 (www.ctc.usma.edu/posts/isils-political-military-power-in-iraq).

7. "Islamic State Turns Radical Islam on Syria Muslims," Reuters, August 26, 2014 (www.reuters.com/article/2014/08/26/us-syria-crisis-province-insight-idUSKBN0GQ1G120140826).

8. Abu Usama, interview by the author, May 2014.

9. "Saddam's Deputy: Baghdad Will Soon Be Liberated," *Al-Arabiya*, July 13, 2014 (http://english.alarabiya.net/en/News/middle-east/2014/07/13/Report-Iraq-s-fugitive-Saddam-era-deputy-praises-ISIS.html).

10. Shane Harris, "The Re-Baathification of Iraq," *Foreign Policy*, August 21, 2014 (www.foreignpolicy.com/articles/2014/08/21/the_re_baathification_of_iraq).

11. Stathis Kalyvas, "The Logic of Violence in the Islamic State's War," *Washington Post*, July 7, 2014 (http://m.washingtonpost.com/blogs/monkey-cage/wp/2014/07/07/the-logic-of-violence-in-islamic-states-war/).

12. Ruth Sherlock, "Inside the Leadership of the Islamic State: How the New Caliphate Is Run," *The Telegraph,* July 9, 2014 (www.telegraph.co.uk/news/worldnews/middleeast/iraq/10956280/Inside-the-leadership-of-Islamic-State-how-the-new-caliphate-is-run.html); Matthew Barber, "New ISIS Leaks Reveal Particulars of Al-Qaida Strategy," *Syria Comment* (blog), January 12, 2014 (www.joshualandis.com/blog/new-isis-leaks-reveal-particulars-of-al-qaida-strategy/); "Exclusive: Top ISIS Leaders Revealed," *Al-Arabiya*, February 13, 2014 (http://english.alarabiya.net/en/News/2014/02/13/Exclusive-Top-ISIS-leaders-revealed.html).

13. Sherlock, "Inside the Leadership."

14. Ibid.

15. Hannah Allam, "Records Show How Iraqi Extremists Withstood U.S. Anti-Terror Efforts," *McClatchy DC*, June 23, 2014 (www.mcclatchydc.com/2014/06/23/231223_records-show-how-iraqi-extremists.html?rh=1).

16. Abu Uthman al-Britani, interview by the author.

17. Ibid.; Allam, "Records Show How Iraqi Extremists Withstood U.S. Anti-Terror Efforts."

18. Barber, "New ISIS Leaks Reveal Particulars."

19. Allam, "Records Show How Iraqi Extremists Withstood U.S. Anti-Terror Efforts."

20. Nour Malas and Maria Abi-Habib, "Islamic State Fills Coffers from Illicit Economy in Syria, Iraq," *Wall Street Journal*, August 27, 2014 (http://online.wsj.com/articles/islamic-state-fills-coffers-from-illicit-economy-in-syria-iraq-1409175458).

21. Keith Johnson, "The Islamic State Is the Newest Petrostate," *Foreign Policy*, July 28, 2014 (www.foreignpolicy.com/articles/2014/07/28/baghdadis_hillbillies_isis_iraq_syria_oil_terrorism_islamic_state).

22. Martin Chulov, "Islamic State Militants Seize Four More Foreign Hostages in Syria," *The Guardian*, August 20, 2014 (www.theguardian.com/world/2014/aug/20/islamic-state-isis-foreign-hostages-syria-aleppo?CMP=twt_gu).

23. "France Denies It Paid Ransom for Syria Reporters," Reuters, April 26, 2014 (www.reuters.com/article/2014/04/26/us-syria-crisis-france-ransom-idUSBREA3P0FE20140426); Raheem Salman and Yara Bayoumy, "Islamic State's Financial Independence Poses Quandary for Its Foes," Reuters, September 11, 2014 (www.reuters.com/article/2014/09/11/us-iraq-crisis-militants-funding-insight-idUSKBN0H60BC20140911?utm_source=twitter).

24. Martin Chulov, "How an Arrest in Iraq Revealed Isis' $2bn Jihadist Network," *The Guardian*, August 15 2014 (www.theguardian.com/world/2014/jun/15/iraq-isis-arrest-jihadists-wealth-power)

25. Mitchell Prothero, "Islamic State Issues Fake Tax Receipts to Keep Trade Flowing," *McClatchy DC*, September 3, 2014 (www.mcclatchydc.com/2014/09/03/238508_islamic-state-issues-fake-tax.html?rh=1).

26. Josh Rogin, "U.S. Ignored Warnings before ISIS Takeover of a Key City," *Daily Beast*, July 10, 2014 (www.thedailybeast.com/articles/2014/07/10/u-s-ignored-warnings-before-isis-takeover-of-a-key-city.html).

27. Interview with IS commander by the author.

28. Interview with official representing units in Rif Dimashq by the author, June 2014.

29. Dan Friedman, "Twitter Stepping Up Suspensions of ISIS-Affiliated Accounts: Experts," *New York Daily News*, August 17, 2014 (www.nydailynews.com/news/world/twitter-stepping-suspensions-isis-affiliated-accounts-experts-article-1.1906193).

30. Lorenzo Francheschi-Bicchierai, "Russia's Facebook Cracks Down on ISIS Accounts," *Mashable*, September 12, 2014 (http://mashable.com/2014/09/12/isis-islamic-state-vkontakte-russia/#:eyJzIjoidCIsImki OiJfcHc2NHByOHE4OHdkNzQybiJ9).

31. Nico Prucja and Ali Fisher, "Is This the Most Successful Release of a Jihadist Video Ever?" *Jihadica* (blog), May 19, 2014 (www.jihad ica.com/is-this-the-most-successful-release-of-a-jihadist-video-ever/).

32. J. M. Berger, "How ISIS Games Twitter," *The Atlantic*, June 16, 2014 (www.theatlantic.com/international/archive/2014/06/isis-iraq-twitter-social-media-strategy/372856/).

33. Cahal Milmo, "ISIS Jihadists Using World Cup and Premier League Hashtags to Promote Propaganda on Twitter," *The Independent*, June 22, 2014 (www.independent.co.uk/news/world/middle-east/iraq-crisis-exclusive-isis-jihadists-using-world-cup-and-premier-league-hashtags-to-promote-extremist-propaganda-on-twitter-9555167.html).

34. Michael W. S. Ryan, "Dabiq: What Islamic State's New Magazine Tells Us about Their Strategic Direction, Recruitment Patterns, and Guerilla Doctrine," *Jamestown Foundation*, August 1, 2014 (www.james town.org/programs/tm/single/?tx_ttnews[tt_news]=42702&cHash =0efbd71af77fb92c064b9403dc8ea838#.U9yARFYpTRp).

35. Greg Miller, "Fighters Abandoning al-Qaeda Affiliates to Join Islamic State, U.S. Officials Say," *Washington Post*, August 9, 2014 (www.washingtonpost.com/world/national-security/fighters-abandoning-al-qaeda-affiliates-to-join-islamic-state-us-officials-say/2014/08/09/c5321d10-1f08-11e4-ae54-0cfe1f974f8a_story.html).

36. Daveed Gartenstein-Ross and Amichai Magen, "The Jihadist Governance Dilemma," *Washington Post*, July 18, 2014 (www.washington post.com/blogs/monkey-cage/wp/2014/07/18/the-jihadist-governance-dilemma/).

37. Goha's Nail [pseud.], "Manbij and the Islamic State's Public Administration," *Jihadology* (blog), August 22, 2014 (http://jihadology. net/2014/08/27/guest-post-manbij-and-the-islamic-states-public-administration/).

38. Jenan Moussa, Twitter post, June 12, 2014 (https://twitter.com/ jenanmoussa/status/477042935821631490/photo/1).

39. See, for example, the Islamic State's *dhimmi* pact in Raqqa, introduced in late February 2014 (http://justpaste.it/ejur).

40. "Convert, Pay Tax, or Die, Islamic State Warns Christians," Reuters, July 18, 2014 (www.theguardian.com/world/2014/jul/18/isis-islamic-state-issue-ultimatum-to-iraq-christians).

41. Cathy Otten, "Last Remaining Christians Flee Iraq's Mosul," *Al Jazeera*, July 22, 2014 (www.aljazeera.com/news/middleeast/2014/ 07/last-remaining-christians-flee-iraq-mosul-201472118235739663.html).

42. "The Revival of Slavery: Before the Hour," *Dabiq,* issue 4, October 2014 (https://ia601403.us.archive.org/0/items/Dabiq04En/ Dabiq_04_en.pdf).

43. "Al-Qaeda in Iraq Alienated by Cucumber Laws and Brutality," *The Telegraph*, August 11, 2008 (www.telegraph.co.uk/news/ worldnews/middleeast/iraq/2538545/Al-Qaeda-in-Iraq-alienated-by-cucumber-laws-and-brutality.html).

44. Hassan Hassan, "Islamic State in Syria, Back with a Vengeance," *Sada*, July 14 2014 (http://carnegieendowment.org/sada/2014/07/14/ islamic-state-in-syria-back-with-vengeance/hfto.

45. Jenna Lefler, "Life under ISIS in Mosul" (Washington: Institute for the Study of War, July 29 2014) (http://iswiraq.blogspot.com/2014/ 07/life-under-isis-in-mosul.html).

46. Aaron Zelin, "The Islamic State of Iraq and Syria Has a Consumer Protection Office," *The Atlantic*, June 13, 2014 (www.theatlantic.com/international/archive/2014/06/the-isis-guide-to-building-an-islamic-state/372769/).

47. "IS Instills Its Own Curriculum in A-Raqqa Schools," *Syria Direct*, September 3, 2014 (http://syriadirect.org/main/37-videos/1537-is-instills-ts-own-curriculum-in-a-raqqa-schools; Sinan Salaheddin and Vivian Salama, "Islamic State Group Issues New Curriculum in Iraq," Associated Press, September 15, 2014 (http://bigstory.ap.org/article/islamic-state-group-issues-new-curriculum-iraq).

48. Abu Dujana, interview by the author.

Chapter 3

1. Kristina Wong, "ISIS Now 'Full-Blown Army,' Officials Warn," *The Hill*, July 23, 2014 (http://thehill.com/policy/defense/213117-us-officials-warn-isis-worse-than-al-qaeda).

2. As outlined in the first issue of the Islamic State's official English-language magazine, *Dabiq*. See "Al-Ḥayāt Media Center Presents a New Issue of the Islamic State's Magazine: 'Dābiq #1,'" *Jihadology* (blog), July 5, 2014 (http://jihadology.net/2014/07/05/al-hayat-media-center-presents-a-new-issue-of-the-islamic-states-magazine-dabiq-1/).

3. Ishaan Tharoor, "A U.S.-Designated Terrorist Group Is Saving Yazidis and Battling the Islamic State," *Washington Post*, August 11, 2014 (www.washingtonpost.com/blogs/worldviews/wp/2014/08/11/a-u-s-designated-terrorist-group-is-saving-yazidis-and-battling-the-islamic-state/).

4. For example, "New Combatants Joined the Islamic State" (Coventry, United Kingdom: Syrian Observatory for Human Rights, September 26, 2014) (http://syriahr.com/en/2014/09/new-combatants-joined-the-islamic-state/).

5. Abu Omar, interview by the author, June 2014.

6. "Islamic State Claims Lebanon Suicide Bombing," Associated Press, June 27, 2014 (http://bigstory.ap.org/article/islamic-state-claims-lebanon-suicide-bombing); "Kahwagi: Army Will Do Utmost to Free Hostages," *Daily Star* (Lebanon), August 12, 2014 (www.dailystar.com.lb/News/Lebanon-News/2014/Aug-12/266928-army-removes-militants-bodies-from-arsal.ashx - axzz3ABS02nte); "Captured Soldiers: They Will Kill Us, If Hezbollah Remains in Syria," *Daily Star* (Lebanon), August 23, 2014 (www.dailystar.com.lb/News/Lebanon-News/2014/Aug-23/268253-captured-soldiers-they-will-kill-us-if-hezbollah-remains-in-syria.ashx#axzz3BDF3z6Ht).

7. William Booth and Taylor Luck, "Jordan Fears Homegrown ISIS More than Invasion from Iraq," *Washington Post*, June 27, 2014 (www.washingtonpost.com/world/middle_east/jordan-fears-home grown-isis-more-than-invasion-from-iraq/2014/06/27/1534a4ee-f48a-492a-99b3-b6cd3ffe9e41_story.html).

8. See, for example, a picture released late on September 26, Charles Lister, Twitter post, September 27, 2014 (https://twitter.com/Charles_Lister/status/515813725706518528/photo/1).

9. Abigail Hauslohner, "Jihadist Expansion in Iraq Puts Persian Gulf States in a Tight Spot," *Washington Post*, June 13, 2014 (www.washingtonpost.com/world/jihadist-expansion-in-iraq-puts-persian-gulf-states-in-a-tight-spot/2014/06/13/e52e90ac-f317-11e3-bf76-447a5df6411f_story.html).

10. Fakhri al-Arashi, "Senior Al-Qaeda Leader Calls for Followers to Support ISIS," *National Yemen*, July 5, 2014 (http://national yemen.com/2014/07/05/senior-al-qaeda-leader-calls-for-followers-to-support-isis/).

11. Ceylan Yeginsu, "ISIS Draws a Steady Stream of Recruits from Turkey," *New York Times*, September 15, 2014 (www.nytimes.com/2014/09/16/world/europe/turkey-is-a-steady-source-of-isis-recruits.html).

12. "I Did a Good Deed by Killing a Turkish Gendarme, Nigde Assailant Says," *Hurriyet Daily News*, March 25, 2014 (www.hurriyet-dailynews.com/i-did-a-good-deed-by-killing-a-turkish-gendarme-nigde-assailant-says.aspx?pageID=238&nID=64060&NewsCatID=341).

13. Omer Faruk Cantenar, interview by the author, July 2014.

14. Aya Elbrqawi, "ISIS Menace al-Qaeda in Derna," *Magharebia*, June 13, 2014 (http://magharebia.com/en_GB/articles/awi/features/2014/06/13/feature-01); J. M. Berger, "The Islamic State vs. al-Qaeda," *Foreign Policy*, September 2, 2014 (www.foreignpolicy.com/articles/2014/09/02/islamic_state_vs_al_qaeda_next_jihadi_super_power).

15. "AQIM Defectors Pledge Loyalty to ISIS," Reuters, September 15, 2014 (www.dailystar.com.lb/News/Middle-East/2014/Sep-15/270689-aqim-defectors-pledge-loyalty-to-isis.ashx#axzz3FRinsX2w); Jonathan Spyer, "Behind the Lines: Under Gaza's Shadow, Islamic State Advances," *Jerusalem Post*, August 3, 2014 (www.jpost.com/Features/Front-Lines/Behind-the-lines-Under-Gazas-shadow-Islamic-State-advances-369670); Patrick Kingsley, "Sinai Jihadist Group Says It Has Beheaded Four Men," *The Guardian*, August 28, 2014 (www.theguardian.com/world/2014/aug/28/sinai-jihaidst-beheads-ansar-beit-al-maqdis).

16. Hamza Idris and Ronald Mutum, "Shekau Proclaims Islamic Caliphate," *Daily Trust*, August 25, 2014 (www.dailytrust.com.ng/daily/top-stories/32604-shekau-proclaims-islamic-caliphate).

17. Ihsanullah Tipu Mehsud and Declan Walsh, "Hardline Splinter Group, Galvanized by ISIS, Emerges from Pakistani Taliban," *New York Times*, August 26, 2014 (www.nytimes.com/2014/08/27/world/asia/hard-line-splinter-group-galvanized-by-isis-emerges-from-pakistani-taliban.html).

18. "BIFF, Abu Sayyaf Pledge Allegiance to Islamic State Jihadists," *GMA Network*, August 16, 2014 (www.gmanetwork.com/news/story/375074/news/nation/biff-abu-sayyaf-pledge-allegiance-to-islamic-state-jihadists).

19. "Jailed Indonesian Terrorist Abu Bakar Bashir Has Been Funding ISIS: Anti-Terrorism Chief," *Straits Times*, July 15, 2014 (www.straitstimes.com/news/asia/south-east-asia/story/jailed-indonesian-terorrist-abu-bakar-bashir-has-been-funding-isis-a).

20. Interviews by the author and tracking of social media; Aaron Zelin, Richard Borrow Fellow at the Washington Institute for Near East Policy, interview by the author, August 2014; Aaron Zelin, "Up to 11,000 Foreign Fighters in Syria; Steep Rise among Western Europeans," *ICSR Insight*, December 2013 (http://icsr.info/2013/12/icsr-insight-11000-foreign-fighters-syria-steep-rise-among-western-europeans/); Brian Bennett and Richard A. Serrano, "More Western Fighters Joining Militants in Iraq and Syria," *Los Angeles Times*, July 19, 2014 (www.latimes.com/world/middleeast/la-fg-foreign-fighters-20140720-story.html#page=1).

21. The previous record was the estimated 5,000–20,000 foreign fighters who traveled to the Afghan jihad over a period of 12 years. Thomas Hegghammer, "The Rise of Muslim Foreign Fighters: Islam and the Globalization of Jihad," *International Security* 35 (Winter 2010–11): 53–94.

22. Chams Eddine Zaougui and Pieter Van Ostaeyen, "Overblown Fears of Foreign Fighters," *New York Times*, July 29, 2014 (www.nytimes.com/2014/07/30/opinion/dont-fear-jihadists-returning-from-syria.html?_r=0).

23. Abu Dujana, interview by the author.

24. Thomas Hegghammer, "Should I Stay or Should I Go? Explaining Variation in Jihadists' Choice between Domestic and Foreign Fighting," *American Political Science Review* 107 (February 2013): 1–15.

25. Adam Taylor, "Could Syria's Islamist Fighters Hit Europe?" *Washington Post*, July 24, 2014 (www.washingtonpost.com/blogs/worldviews/wp/2014/07/24/could-syrias-islamist-fighters-hit-europe/).

26. Mehdi Nemmouche, charged with killing four people at the Jewish Museum of Belgium in Brussels on May 24, 2014, is suspected

of having spent over twelve months fighting in Syria and of having been a member of the Islamic State. Tamerlan Tsarnaev, one of two brothers involved in the Boston Marathon bombings on April 15, 2013, had spent time in the Russian North Caucasus republic of Dagestan in 2012, where the FBI claims he spent time at a mosque in Makhachkala believed to espouse "radical Islam." Michael Adebolajo, one of two men responsible for the murder of an off-duty British soldier in London on May 22, 2013, was arrested in Kenya in 2010 while allegedly seeking military training with Harakat Al-Shabaab al-Mujahideen.

27. Umberto Bacchi, "France: ISIS Jihadi Mehdi Nemmouche to Be Extradited over Brussels Jewish Museum Attack," *International Business Times*, June 26, 2014 (www.ibtimes.co.uk/france-isis-jihadist-mehdi-nemmouche-be-extradited-over-brussels-jewish-museum-attack-1454356); Paul Cruickshank, "Raid on ISIS Suspect in the French Riviera," *CNN*, August 28, 2014 (http://edition.cnn.com/2014/08/28/world/europe/france-suspected-isis-link/).

28. Michael Holden, "Top UK Anti-Terrorism Official Says Syria-Related Arrests Soar," Reuters, August 26 2014 (http://uk.reuters.com/article/2014/08/26/uk-iraq-security-foley-britain-idUKKBN0GQ1IP20140826); "UK Terror Threat Raised to 'Severe,'" *BBC News*, August 29, 2014 (www.bbc.com/news/uk-28986271).

29. Aaron Zelin, "Syria: The Epicenter of Future Jihad," *Policywatch* 2278 (Washington Institute for Near East Policy, June 30, 2014) (www.washingtoninstitute.org/policy-analysis/view/26142).

30. Yara Bayoumy, "Islamic State Urges Attacks on U.S., French Citizens, Taunts Obama," Reuters, September 22, 2014 (www.reuters.com/article/2014/09/22/us-iraq-crisis-adnani-idUSKCN0HH1MB20140922).

31. Steve Grudgings and Trinna Long, "Malaysian Militants Bought Bomb Material for Planned Attack—Official," Reuters, August 21, 2014 (www.reuters.com/article/2014/08/21/us-malaysia-islamicstate-idUSKBN0GL0BQ20140821).

32. Chip Le Grand, "Teen Terrorist Abdul Numan Haider May Not Have Acted Alone: Police," *The Australian*, September 25, 2014 (www.theaustralian.com.au/in-depth/terror/teen-terrorist-abdul-numan-haider-may-not-have-acted-alone-police/story-fnpdbcmu-1227070024066); Shane Green, "The Young Faces of Terror," *Sydney Morning Herald*, September 27, 2014 (www.smh.com.au/national/the-young-faces-of-terror-20140926-10mf9v.html).

33. Interview by the author, June 2014.

34. Interview by the author with a member of the al-Ittihad al-Islami Ajnad al-Sham alliance based in Damascus, June 2014.

35. Mitchell Prothero, "Expansion of 'Secret' Facility in Iraq Suggests Closer US-Kurd Ties," *McClatchy DC*, July 11, 2014 (www.miami herald.com/2014/07/11/4231510/expansion-of-secret-facility-in.html).

36. Interview with a Shai'tat leader by the author, August 2014.

Index

Surnames beginning with al- are alphabetized by the part of the name that follows.